AAT

Q2022

LEVEL 2

End Point Assessment

EXAM KIT

This Exam Kit supports study for the following AAT qualifications:
AAT Level 2 Certificate in Accounting
AAT Level 2 Certificate in Bookkeeping
AAT Certificate in Accounting at SCQF Level 6

KAPLAN
PUBLISHING

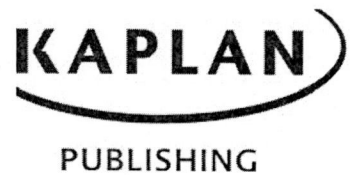

AAT: L2 END POINT ASSESSMENT

British Library Cataloguing-in-Publication Data

A catalogue record for this book is available from the British Library.

Published by:

Kaplan Publishing UK
Unit 2 The Business Centre
Molly Millar's Lane
Wokingham
Berkshire
RG41 2QZ

ISBN: 978-1-83996-510-4

© Kaplan Financial Limited, 2023

Printed and bound in Great Britain.

The text in this material and any others made available by any Kaplan Group company does not amount to advice on a particular matter and should not be taken as such. No reliance should be placed on the content as the basis for any investment or other decision or in connection with any advice given to third parties. Please consult your appropriate professional adviser as necessary. Kaplan Publishing Limited and all other Kaplan group companies expressly disclaim all liability to any person in respect of any losses or other claims, whether direct, indirect, incidental, consequential or otherwise arising in relation to the use of such materials.

All rights reserved. No part of this examination may be reproduced or transmitted in any form or by any means, electronic or mechanical, including photocopying, recording, or by any information storage and retrieval system, without prior permission from Kaplan Publishing.

CONTENTS

	Page
EPA Overview	P.4
Assessment method 1	P.5
Assessment method 2	P.7
Index to questions and answers	P.9
Exam technique	P.10

Practice questions	1
Answers to practice questions	59
Mock assessment questions	91
Mock assessment answers	111

Features in this exam kit

In addition to providing a wide ranging bank of real exam style questions, we have also included in this kit:

- unit-specific information and advice on exam technique

You will find a wealth of other resources to help you with your studies on the AAT website:

www.aat.org.uk/

Quality and accuracy are of the utmost importance to us so if you spot an error in any of our products, please send an email to mykaplanreporting@kaplan.com with full details, or follow the link to the feedback form in MyKaplan.

Our Quality Co-ordinator will work with our technical team to verify the error and take action to ensure it is corrected in future editions.

KAPLAN PUBLISHING

EPA OVERVIEW

The objective of this EPA is to ensure full competency as an Accounts/Finance Assistant.

The apprenticeship provides a basis for progression into a number of career paths in the accounting sector including Assistant Financial Accountant, Payroll Manager, Senior Finance Officer or Payments and Billing Manager.

Once the apprentice has completed the Assistant Accountant apprenticeship, fulfilling the OPL and EPA requirements, they could take on the following job roles:

- Accounts Assistant
- Accounts Payable Clerk
- Accounts Administrator
- Business Accounts Administrator
- Finance Assistant Junior
- Cost Accountant
- Assistant Bookkeeper
- Junior Cashier
- Junior Credit Control Clerk
- Data Input Clerk
- Accounts Receivable Clerk
- Cash Poster
- Finance Administrator

Below is an overview of the two assessments:

Assessment method	Area assessed	Assessed by	Grading
Structured interview (supported by portfolio of evidence summary)	1. Teamwork 2. Professionalism 3. Customer focus 4. Ethical standards 5. General business 6. Understanding your organisation 7. Personal effectiveness 8. Communication 9. Personal development 10. Uses systems and processes	End Point Assessment Organisation (EPAO)	Fail/Pass/ Distinction
Intray-test	1. Accounting systems and processes 2. Basic accounting 3. Attention to detail	End Point Assessment Organisation (EPAO)	Fail/Pass

ASSESSMENT METHOD 1

STRUCTURED INTERVIEW (SUPPORTED BY THE SUMMARY OF PORTFOLIO EVIDENCE)

In preparation for the structured interview, the apprentice will produce a portfolio of evidence that will be signed off by the employer as part of the gateway requirements. Although the portfolio does not contribute towards the overall grade, apprentices must submit to AAT, within two weeks of the gateway and at least one month before the scheduled EPA, a sufficient summary of competence against each knowledge, skill and behaviour assessed in the structured interview. The Portfolio must contain a minimum of four pieces of evidence that when cross-referenced, sufficiently demonstrate competence against all requirements.

The typical elements of the portfolio are:

- job related certificates
- observation report undertaken by a third party (e.g. a workplace mentor)
- completed observation checklist and related action plans
- worksheets, assignment projects and reports
- record of any formal discussions (e.g. professional discussion, performance review)
- record of oral and written questioning
- apprentice and peer reports.

Structured interview

The structured interview must last for 60 minutes. The independent assessor has the discretion to increase the time of the structured interview by up to 10% to allow the apprentice to complete their last answer. Further time may be granted for apprentices with appropriate needs, for example where signing services are required. The structured interview will be conducted as set out here:

The structured interview will focus on the portfolio completed by the apprentice during the on-programme phase of the Apprenticeship, and the independent assessor will seek to gain assurance of the apprentice's competency by questioning. The independent assessor will receive the Portfolio within 2 weeks of the gateway.

The independent assessor will draw 10 questions from AAT's question bank to ask the apprentice. All 10 questions will be asked.

The independent assessor may ask any number of their own additional follow up questions within the total time permitted for the structured interview to delve deeper into the apprentice's answers if this is necessary to authenticate evidence, experience and competence. The apprentice may refer to their Portfolio during the discussion should they wish to.

A structured specification and question bank will be developed by AAT. The 'question bank' will be of sufficient size to prevent predictability and we will review it regularly (and at least once a year) to ensure that it, and its content, are fit for purpose. The specifications, including questions relating to the underpinning knowledge, skills and behaviours, will be varied yet allow assessment of the relevant KSBs. AAT will ensure that apprentices have a different set of questions in the case of re-sits/re-takes.

The interview with the apprentice will be conducted remotely via the AAT EPA software system called Smart End Point Assessment (SEPA).

For the structured interview:

- Our questions will seek to assess competence and/or depth of understanding to assess performance. Clarification questioning is permitted to explore the apprentice's given answers to the prepared questions.

- We will schedule the interview to take place at an agreed time and place, giving both the apprentice and the independent assessor a minimum of two weeks' notice of the time, date and venue.

- The interview should take place on a one-to-one basis between an independent assessor and an apprentice via the prescribed method.

- The interview must take place in a quiet room away from workplace distraction and influence.

- AAT will specify any equipment and software required for the interview.

- AAT will ensure any reasonable adjustments are in place and apprentices must make any requirement requests at least 1 week prior to the scheduled date for the interview.

- Independent assessors will record apprentice's responses against the knowledge, skills and behaviours via pre-prepared template forms to ensure that due process has been followed. Appeals will only be reviewed against documented evidence against the pass and distinction criteria.

- Independent assessors will assess the interview and award a fail, pass or distinction grade to AAT.

- AAT will create a report template for the assessor to submit to confirm the grade.

ASSESSMENT METHOD 2

IN-TRAY TEST

The test provides for an in-tray exercise based on a fictitious organisation's scenario, which replicates the typical work an Accounts/Finance Assistant will have to manage in a workplace.

By its very nature, the Accounts/Finance Assistant occupation demands accurate and detailed written work, including calculations, and so this assessment method is an appropriate and manageable way of testing occupational competency against the knowledge and skills requirements.

The scenarios will be based on a variety of different organisational structures or operations and success will require an integration of the technical knowledge and skills required for the standard.

Test format

The test will be computer based. The test will consist of a combination of questions and data evaluations that cover the knowledge and skills identified as applicable to this assessment method within the grading criteria.

At the start of the in-tray test, in invigilated conditions, the apprentice will be presented with the equivalent of three A4 pieces of background information (with a word count of up to 1500 words) about one particular scenario.

Each scenario will represent the casework and likely situations the apprentice will encounter in their work.

The scenario will be concise and will include:

- Details of the organisation – (name and address of business, type of business (sole trader, partnership, limited company etc.), details of the organisation's VAT registration (VAT number, whether the business uses the standard or cash VAT system), the services the organisation offers (including details of the rates of applicable VAT).

- Recording costs – How the organisation records its costs. For example, if the organisation is a service or retail organisation, it may contain relevant details of any stock system utilised so that the apprentice can understand the nature of how these costs are recorded and used. A list of expense/overhead accounts will be given to allow the apprentice to understand the format of the organisation's chart of accounts and to understand how such costs are recorded. If the organisation records details of costs against projects, then details will be provided

- Task – The scenario will also include brief details of the role the apprentice will be assuming during the assessment to enable them to understand the limits of their responsibilities and at which point any queries or concerns should be referred upwards within the organisation. It will also give some idea of the controls that are operated within the organisation.

The scenario will first require the apprentice to answer 20 multiple choice questions along the following themes:

- how accounting systems and processes allows the fictitious organisation to keep track of all types of financial transaction
- accounts reports, reports and their use within the finance function
- bookkeeping controls
- recognise and rectifies errors.

Secondly, there will be 3 short answer questions that require the apprentice to provide their written answers to the following factors relating to the scenario:

- the internal controls within the fictitious organisation
- the cost recording system within the fictitious organisation
- the differences between Financial and Management Accounting within the fictious organization.

No word count is specified; instead the apprentice's answers will be limited to the overall time available for the entire in-tray test.

The third and final part of the in-tray test requires the apprentice to consider the data they have been provided alongside the background information relating to the fictitious organisation. This will cover basic accountancy concepts and double entry bookkeeping alongside the ability to examine data to identify issues and the ability to reconcile data to minimise the chance of errors. The scenario will provide the opportunity for the apprentice to identify and rectify at least 3 data related errors.

The apprentice will be asked to enter the data into an IT data entry facility. Documents could be invoices, credit notes or receipt/payment transactions.

The apprentice is expected to select the correct details for transactions, such as general ledger codes, VAT rates, Net, VAT and gross amounts. They must also be able to show the final result of the posting in the accounts – for example, how this would show in a mini trial balance.

One possible scenario could be to provide a trial balance that contains errors. There could be notes to the accounts that give errors such as reversed digits in an entry, an account balance that appears in the wrong column, etc. The apprentice should be able to find the errors and complete a new trial balance, giving totals.

Time allowed

The total assessment duration is 1 hour and 45 minutes. This **includes 15 minutes** reading time to review the scenario. You may use this time to make notes to help you prepare. You will have 1 hour and 30 minutes to respond to all tasks.

PASS MARK

The minimum marks needed for a pass are 75 out of 100.

 Always keep your eye on the clock and make sure you attempt all questions!

DETAILED SYLLABUS

The detailed syllabus and study guide written by the AAT can be found at: www.aat.org.uk/

INDEX TO QUESTIONS AND ANSWERS

		Page number	
		Question	Answer
Scenario 1	Keep It Clean	1	59
Scenario 2	Diggit	20	69
Scenario 3	Blue BBQ	38	80

	Question	Answer
MOCK ASSESSMENT		
Questions	91	
Answers		111

EXAM TECHNIQUE

- **Do not skip any of the material** in the syllabus.
- **Read each question very** carefully.
- **Double-check your answer** before committing yourself to it.
- Answer **every** question – if you do not know an answer to a multiple choice question or true/false question, you don't lose anything by guessing. Think carefully before you **guess**.
- If you are answering a multiple-choice question, **eliminate first those answers that you know are wrong.** Then choose the most appropriate answer from those that are left.
- **Don't panic** if you realise you've answered a question incorrectly. Getting one question wrong will not mean the difference between passing and failing.

Computer-based exams – tips

- Do not attempt a CBA until you have **completed all study material** relating to it.
- On the AAT website there is a CBA demonstration. It is **ESSENTIAL** that you attempt this before your real CBA. You will become familiar with how to move around the CBA screens and the way that questions are formatted, increasing your confidence and speed in the actual exam.
- Be sure you understand how to use the **software** before you start the exam. If in doubt, ask the assessment centre staff to explain it to you.
- Questions are **displayed on the screen** and answers are entered using keyboard and mouse. At the end of the exam, in the case of those units not subject to human marking, you are given a certificate showing the result you have achieved.
- In addition to the traditional multiple-choice question type, CBAs will also contain **other types of questions**, such as number entry questions, drag and drop, true/false, pick lists or drop down menus or hybrids of these.
- In some CBAs you will have to type in complete computations or written answers.
- You need to be sure you **know how to answer questions** of this type before you sit the exam, through practice.

Section 1

PRACTICE QUESTIONS

SCENARIO 1

Keep it Clean

13 Squeeky Street

Ethicstown

ET15 6WE

VAT registration 978 51349 94

Background information

Keep it Clean is owned by Charlene Otter, a sole trader. The business manufactures ethical clothing. The majority of the clothing is sold to department stores but a small number of sales are made to the general public at ethical fashion events. The fashion items are produced in a local factory and there is an office on-site where all the administration and distribution is managed.

The office, factory and warehouse are owned by Keep it Clean, but the delivery vehicles are rented under short-term leases of 12 months with the annual rental charge agreed each year. The rental charge includes all general repair costs associated with the vehicles but not the mileage or any damage caused by the Keep it Clean drivers.

Payroll information

The factory manager and office staff are paid an annual salary. The factory workers are paid an hourly rate and generally work 40 hours each week, although overtime is available if approved by the factory manager. There is high staff turnover in the factory and employees are often employed at short notice to meet demand, meaning payments are often made without supporting documentation.

The majority of the sales staff in the office receive a set wage plus commission for any new orders they have generated.

Event sales staff work solely at the ethical fashion events. These are paid an hourly rate and can vary dependent on the length of the event. These events are sometimes on national holidays, and the wages on these attract a 40% premium on the hourly rate. It is up to the event staff to record if they worked on a national holiday or not.

The factory workers submit weekly timesheets to the Finance Department. The finance department process this through payroll, checking for evidence of authorisation of any overtime worked.

The sales manager submits a monthly report to the Finance Director at the end of every month, with details of new orders generated by each member of the sales team in that month in order for the commission to be calculated correctly as part of the monthly payroll. All payroll figures are prepared and authorised by Gigi Osborne, the finance manager.

Finance department

You are Tunde Gomis and work for Keep it Clean as a Finance Assistant. Today's date is 1 October 20XX. Your team consists of yourself and two other Finance Assistants called Emma James and Jimmy Houston and you all report to your line manager, Gigi Osborne. Gigi performs a monthly check of the balances on the receivables ledger against the agreed credit limit of customers.

Gigi has just completed the following reports to send to the Finance Director:

- A statement of profit or loss for the period ended 30 September 20XX
- The budgeted staff costs for the factory for November and December
- An assessment of returns of poor-quality materials to suppliers during the period.

VAT

The organisation operates the standard VAT scheme. All sales are subject to VAT at the standard rate, other than clothes for children, which have a zero rate of VAT. The VAT rate for purchases and expenses is determined by the type of supply.

Accounting system

Keep it Clean uses a customised digital bookkeeping system. There is a rota system used by you, Emma and Jimmy to do daily checks on the entries made.

All bank receipts and payments and petty cash receipts and payments are entered manually into a cash book/petty cash book. The bank columns of the manual cash book are reconciled with the bank statement on a monthly basis. Gigi keeps the petty cash box on her desk and reimburses an expense when she receives a receipt. All journals are recorded in a journal daybook.

Once a transaction is entered into the digital bookkeeping system, the system will automatically post entries to all relevant accounts. When a journal to write off an irrecoverable debt is entered, the system will also make the necessary adjustment to that particular customer's account in the receivables ledger.

Transactions are entered into the digital bookkeeping system by selecting menu options. Payments to credit suppliers and receipts from credit customers are recorded using the Credit suppliers and Credit customer's menu options. All other payments and receipts are recorded according to the payment method.

PRACTICE QUESTIONS: **SECTION 1**

These are the menu options you may need to use today:

Main menu	**Sub menu**
Credit suppliers	Purchase invoices
	Purchase credit notes
	Payments to credit suppliers
Credit customers	Sales invoices
	Sales credit notes
	Receipts from credit customers
Bank	Payments
	Receipts
Cash	Payments
	Receipts
Petty cash	Payments
	Receipts
General ledger	Journal entries

These are the accounting codes you may need to use today:

General ledger code	Account	General ledger code	Account
001	Sales – adult clothes	601	Rent paid
002	Sales – children's clothes	602	Repairs and maintenance
003	Sales – fashion events	603	Gas expense
004	Discounts allowed	604	Electricity expense
005	Purchases	605	Telephone expense
006	Discounts received	606	Motor expenses
101	Bank	607	Water rates
102	Cash in hand	608	Accountancy fees
103	Petty cash	609	Legal fees
201	Factory wages	610	Sundry expenses
202	Office wages	611	Insurance
203	Other salaries	612	Subsistence
204	HMRC liability	613	Bank charges and interest
205	Pension liability	614	Irrecoverable debts written off
402	Receivables ledger control	701	Capital
403	VAT control	702	Drawings
501	Land and buildings		
502	Motor vehicles		
503	Fixtures and fittings		
504	Plant and machinery		

Payroll information

The payroll details for the sales staff are as follows:

Name of employee	Employee code	Monthly salary	Commission percentage
Nish Syal	2143	£2,300.00	30%
James Gamble	2342	£2,100.00	22%
Ed Acaster	2566	£1,875.00	22%
Alexandra Key	2857	£1,400.00	18%
Jessica Horne	2858	£1,280.00	18%

The payroll details for the event sales staff are as follows:

Name of employee	Employee code	Hourly rate
Keri Knappett	2167	£16.60
Romesh Chaudry	2293	£15.20
Kevin Chan	2701	£14.50
Fern Watson	2804	£13.00

Other information

Charlene is keen to expand the business by attending more ethical fashion events in the run-up to Christmas. In order to do this, she will need to invest more money into the business and employ more events staff.

During your recent appraisal you expressed a keen interest in the payroll function of the business. Gigi agreed that as part of your professional development, she would delegate the task of checking the payroll to you.

Keep it Clean requires all accounting staff to have up-to-date knowledge in the areas of accounting systems and processes, bookkeeping controls and the recognition and rectification of errors.

Staff must periodically complete a test comprising 13 questions to evidence their continuing professional development in these areas. You have been asked to complete the test today.

PRACTICE QUESTIONS: SECTION 1

TASK 1

(a) Which of the following is not a routine task?

Tasks	
Checking all orders have been delivered	
Checking the condition of goods sent to a customer	
Sending sales invoices when goods are delivered	
Performing an analysis of whether any companies are breaching their payment terms	

(b) Which item is classified as a non-current asset of Keep it Clean?

Item	
Factory owned by Keep it Clean	
Delivery vehicles rented by Keep it Clean	
Keep it Clean's bank account	
Inventory of clothing for sale	

(c) Which item is classified as an expense of Keep it Clean?

Item	
A debt written off in relation to a customer	
Drawings by the owner of the business	
Cash put into the business by the owner	
Items returned by a customer	

(d) If Keep It Clean always tops up petty cash to the same amount, what is the name of this system?

System	
Voucher system	
Constant float method	
Imprest system	
Reimbursement method	

TASK 2

(a) Which of these documents would be issued by Keep it Clean to a customer who has returned clothes due to poor quality?

Document	
Sales invoice	
Credit note	
Debit note	
Remittance advice	

(b) Each customer of Keep it Clean is given a code made up of numbers, with the number increasing each time a new customer is registered. What type of code is this?

Type of code	
Alphanumeric	
Faceted	
Sequential	
Alphabetical	

(c) Which of the following benefits is true in respect of a coding system?

Benefits of coding system	
It reduces the time taken to find transactions	
It helps categorise items by class	
It can help to reduce errors	
All of the above	

(d) What document is often sent with a customer's payment to inform the company which items are being paid?

Document	
Debit note	
Payment slip	
Quotation	
Remittance advice	

PRACTICE QUESTIONS: SECTION 1

TASK 3

(a) Which of the following accounts would not be affected by a credit sale of adult's clothes?

Account	
Cash	
Sales	
VAT	
Trade receivables	

(b) If a customer with an outstanding balance relating to adult clothes is declared bankrupt, which of the following accounts would not be affected in recording this?

Account	
614 Irrecoverable debts written off	
402 Receivables ledger control	
001 Sale – adult clothes	
403 VAT control	

(c) When a credit customer makes a payment for an outstanding balance owed in respect of children's clothes, taking advantage of an early payment discount, which of the following isn't recorded in the entries?

Entries	
Deduct from receivables	
Include in cash	
Include in sales	
Record a discount allowed	

(d) Which of the following would not be a reason for the difference between the balance on the receivables ledger control account and the total of the receivables ledger balances?

Reason	
Discounts allowed were recorded in the ledger balances but not the control account	
A late sale was only recorded in the control account	
A sale of £630 was recorded as £360 in both the control account and ledger accounts	
Payments received were recorded at £410 in the control account and £400 in the receivables ledger balances	

TASK 4

(a) In addition to gross wages, which of the items below would be included in Keep it Clean's wages expense?

Wages expense	
Employee charitable deductions	
PAYE deductions	
Employer's NIC	
Employee's NIC	

(b) Which of these items would explain why an employee's net pay is different to their gross pay?

Item	
Bonus payments	
Paid annual leave	
Overtime payments	
PAYE deductions	

(c) If Gigi prepares the payroll calculations and authorises the payroll, what risk does this process present?

Issue	
Risk of fraud due to lack of segregation of duties	
It is illegal for Gigi to do if she is not a qualified accountant	
Payroll should be done by someone more senior than Gigi	
Payroll must be done by external people, not employees	

(d) You have been asked to calculate Nish Sayal's net pay. In addition to his monthly salary, he also won a new contract worth £5,000 and his normal commission rate applies. Relevant NIC and PAYE figures are as follows:

Monthly PAYE	£592
Monthly employee's NIC & pension	£315
Monthly employer's NIC & pension	£512

What is Nish's net pay this month?

Amount	
£2,381	
£2,893	
£3,405	
£1,393	

PRACTICE QUESTIONS: SECTION 1

TASK 5

(a) Keep it Clean sells 100 items of adult clothing for £12 each plus VAT at 20%, offering a 5% trade discount to its customer.

Which of the following correctly shows the gross amount on the invoice?

Amount	
£1,440	
£1,380	
£1,428	
£1,368	

(b) Jimmy has prepared an invoice for £1,680 including VAT at 20%.

What is the amount that Keep it Clean can record in sales in respect of this transaction?

Amount	
£1,344	
£2,016	
£1,400	
£1,680	

(c) At the end of the month, Keep it Clean must pay HMRC £3,000 in respect of VAT owed.

What is the correct double entry to record this payment?

Entry	
Dr Bank, Cr VAT	
Dr VAT, Cr Bank	
Dr Sales, Cr VAT	
Dr VAT, Cr Sales	

(d) Which of the following is considered a feature of a digital bookkeeping system?

Transaction	
It is a backup of physical records	
It doesn't require a password to access the system	
It is a system which stores accounting records online	
It removes the need for bank payments to be authorised	

TASK 6

As the finance team has grown Gigi Osborne has been very keen to implement bookkeeping controls.

(a) Identify TWO internal controls already in place in respect of payroll at Keep it Clean.

Gigi would like to introduce even more controls over the payroll system.

(b) Identify THREE internal controls that could be introduced to help improve the payroll system.

PRACTICE QUESTIONS: **SECTION 1**

TASK 7

Gigi has sent her reports to the Finance Director.

(a) Identify which report from Gigi is not classified as a management accounting report.

(b) Identify THREE other major elements of non-payroll costs that would be incurred by Keep it Clean and could be included in a budget of total company expenses.

(c) State ONE example of how the Finance Director may use the information in Gigi's report of returns to each supplier.

TASK 8

Keep it Clean classifies costs in different ways.

(a) Explain what is meant by an indirect cost.

(b) Identify one fixed cost incurred by Keep it Clean.

(c) State TWO costs incurred by Keep it Clean which are indirect costs.

PRACTICE QUESTIONS: SECTION 1

TASK 9

Emma has checked the weekly timesheet from an event staff employee below:

Employee Name: Romesh Chaudry Timesheet number: 1167					Employee Code: 2293
Date	Day of week	Time started	Time ended	Breaks (minutes)	Total hours
11.09.XX	Monday	08:00	17:00	60	8
12.09.XX	Tuesday	10:00	14:30	60	3.5
14.09.XX	Thursday	09:00	14:30	30	5
16.09.XX	Saturday	09:30	17:30	120	6
					22.5

Upon further discovery, you have noted that Monday was a national holiday.

(a) Enter the timesheet into the digital bookkeeping system by:

– selecting the appropriate menu option

– entering the details of the timesheet

Menu option

Picklist: Bank – Payments, Cash – Payments, Petty Cash – Payments, General ledger – journal entries

Employee code	Timesheet number	Number of hours	Rate	Rate per hour
	1167			
	1167			

Picklist: Normal rate, Overtime rate

You have been supplied with the following figures for the monthly wage bill for the factory:

Item	£
Gross wages	45,000
Employer's NIC	5,610
Employee's NIC	3,820
PAYE	9,400
Employer pension contribution	2,600
Employee pension contribution	1,500

(b) Show how the wages expense will be recorded in the general ledger.

Account name	Amount £	Debit	Credit

Picklist: Wages expense, HMRC liability, Pension liability, Wages control, Bank

TASK 10

Emma has received information regarding new contracts which qualify for commission in respect of two of the sales team below:

Employee	Employee code	Sales made £
James Gamble	2342	1,600
Jessica Horne	2858	2,300

(a) Complete the entries below by inserting:

- the monthly salary for each individual
- the amount of commission each staff member should receive

Sales staff commission schedule

Employee	Employee code	Salary £	Commission £
James Gamble	2342		
Jessica Horne	2858		

You have been given the invoice below relating to a credit purchase:

Cott On

VAT registration 446 1552 01

Invoice number 1923

To: Keep it Clean   28 September 20XX

	£
40 of product code 45 @ £6.50 each	260.00
VAT @ 20%	52.00
Total	312.00

Upon receipt of the goods, you have discovered that 10 of the items were damaged and need returning.

(b) Record the double entry required to account for the purchase return.

Debit/credit	Account (Picklist)	Amount £
Dr		
Cr		
Cr		

Picklist: Purchases, Purchase returns, VAT, Trade payables, Sales

PRACTICE QUESTIONS: SECTION 1

TASK 11

You have informed Gigi that the payables ledger control account shows an amount of £14,620 owing to suppliers. You find that a contra with a customer for £400 needs to be made.

(a) What will be the balance brought down in the payables ledger control account after you have entered this transaction, and will it be a debit or credit?

Amount £	Debit/Credit

Picklist: Debit, Credit

Having made several entries into the digital bookkeeping system you are checking your input when you notice an error. A cash sale of adult clothes of £250 plus VAT of 20% was incorrectly recorded as a cash purchase.

(b) Select the correct general ledger codes and prepare entries in the journal daybook to:

– remove the incorrect entries

– record the correct entries

Journal daybook

General ledger code (picklist)	Debit £	Credit £
Details: journal to remove the incorrect entries		

Picklist: 001, 002, 004, 005, 101, 102, 103, 403

General ledger code (picklist)	Debit £	Credit £
Details: journal to record the correct entries		

Picklist: 001, 002, 004, 005, 101, 102, 103, 403

AAT: L2 END POINT ASSESSMENT

TASK 12

Jimmy has started work on the monthly bank reconciliation process. He has sent you the note below, the latest bank statement and an extract from the cash book.

Note from Jimmy:

> I was working through the bank statement checks against the cash book but have run out of time and haven't managed to complete this before I go on annual leave tomorrow. I have made the entry into the cash book for the interest received.
>
> I think there must be some reconciling items but I have not had time to work these out. Could you identify these and complete the bank reconciliation for me please?

Bank statement

Nateast Bank PLC

To: Keep it Clean   Account No: 52354861

Statement of Account

Date 20XX	Detail	Paid out £	Paid in £	Balance £	
01 Sept	Balance b/d			11,240	C
01 Sept	Cheque 110156	500		10,740	C
01 Sept	Bank credit Smith		180	10,920	C
01 Sept	Interest received		120	11,040	C
11 Sept	Cheque 110157	390		10,650	C
12 Sept	Cheque 110159	240		10,410	C
13 Sept	Cheque 110161	400		10,010	C
15 Sept	Bank credit Maher		990	11,000	C
17 Sept	Paid in to Nateast Bank PLC		850	11,850	C
23 Sept	Direct debit electricity	300		11,550	C
23 Sept	Interest received		100	11,650	C
D = Debit C = Credit					

PRACTICE QUESTIONS: SECTION 1

Cash book

Date 20XX	Details	Bank £	Date 20XX	Cheque number	Details	Bank £
01 Sept	Balance b/d	10,740	07 Sept	110157	Waterfall	390
1 Sept	Smith	180	07 Sept	110158	Crocombe	600
14 Sept	Event sales	850	07 Sept	110159	Efete	240
16 Sept	Maher	990	07 Sept	110160	Glennon	1,060
22 Sept	McAtee	500	07 Sept	110161	Amos	400
20 Sept	Holahan	1,030	23 Sept	DD	Electricity	300
22 Sept	Event sales	520				
01 Sept	Interest received	120				
23 Sept	Interest received	100				

(a) What is the balance carried down in the cash book?

£	Debit/credit

Picklist: Debit, Credit

You have identified some errors in Jimmy's note regarding the bank reconciliation.

(b) Complete the bank reconciliation statement as at 23 June.

Note: Do not make any entries in the shaded boxes.

Bank reconciliation statement as at 23 June 20XX

Balance per bank statement	
Outstanding lodgements (name)	
Unpresented cheques (number)	
Balance as per cash book	

KAPLAN PUBLISHING

17

TASK 13

Gigi has forwarded you the following information from Charlene relating to the expansion of the ethical fashion events side of the business.

> Hi Gigi,
>
> We really believe that the ethical fashion part of the business is the future, and so I am investing money to build that side of things. I have put a further £30,000 of my own money into the company bank account for this purpose. Of that, £5,000 has already been spent on advertising in a fashion magazine.
>
> Can you process these entries for me please?
>
> Thanks, Charlene

(a) Prepare entries in the journal daybook to record the injection of cash and advertising in the fashion magazine.

Journal daybook

Account name	Debit £	Credit £
Details: Journal to record the cash injection		

Picklist: 001, 002, 101, 102, 701, 702

Account name	Debit £	Credit £
Details: Journal to record the advertisement		

Picklist: 001, 002, 101, 102, 610, 611

Emma would like to know why money Charlene withdraws for her personal usage is not an expense to the business.

(b) Which of the following principles will you use to explain this to Emma?

Accounting principle	
Accounting equation	
Business entity	
Dual aspect	

PRACTICE QUESTIONS: SECTION 1

Emma is also looking at a summary of items in the records of Keep it Clean, and is unsure whether these are recorded in assets, liabilities or capital.

(c) Using the information from the list below, total the amounts to be recorded in assets, liabilities and capital.

Item	Amount £
Owned equipment	18,000
Bank account	27,000
Loan owed to bank	13,000
Money injected by Charlene	30,000
Receivables ledger control	8,000

Assets £	Liabilities £	Capital £

KAPLAN PUBLISHING

AAT: L2 END POINT ASSESSMENT

SCENARIO 2

Diggit

1 Churny Close

Farmville

FV34 4RZ

VAT registration 978 13549 92

Background information

Diggit is owned by Rick Greene, a sole trader. The business sells garden and barbecue equipment to garden centres. In addition, Diggit holds family events where families pay to ride on specially customised diggers on local farmland. The equipment is produced at a local factory and there is an office on-site where all the administration and distribution is managed. There is a local warehouse where all the equipment is stored when completed.

The office and factory are owned by Diggit, but the warehouse is rented under a short-term lease of 12 months with the annual rental charge agreed each year. The rental charge includes all utility bills for the warehouse.

The factory manager and office staff are paid an annual salary. The factory workers are paid an hourly rate of £10 an hour and generally work 40 hours each week. The factory workers submit weekly timesheets to the Finance Department who then process this through payroll. Some experienced factory staff with specialised licences also work solely at the family events as drivers. These are paid an additional hourly rate of £14 an hour. The events are sometimes on national holidays, and the wages on these attracts a 30% premium on the hourly rate.

The majority of the sales staff in the office receive a set wage plus commission for any orders from new customers. The sales manager submits a monthly report to the Finance Director at the end of every month, with details of new orders generated by each member of the sales team in that month.

In terms of new customers, all of these are subject to a credit check. This is performed by the sales staff and reviewed by the sales manager. Once these credit checks are performed, the customer is given a sequentially numbered code. No other controls are deemed necessary other than the finance manager confirming that all sales with commission do relate to customers that were not present in the previous month.

You are Michonne Negan and work for Diggit as a Finance Assistant. Today's date is 1 May 20XX. Your team consists of you and two other Finance Assistants called Rosita Porter and Morgan Ford and you all report to your line manager, Maggie Grimes.

VAT

The organisation operates the standard VAT scheme. The VAT rate for purchases and expenses is determined by the type of supply.

Reports

Maggie Grimes prepares the statement of financial position and statement of profit or loss for the year, in addition to VAT returns for HMRC.

Various other department heads produce other useful reports aimed at improving the performance of Diggit.

The factory manager produces a report of units produced each week, in addition to the amount of downtime due to damaged machinery. The warehouse supervisor produces a report showing the outstanding orders not delivered at the end of each week. The purchasing team also runs a monthly report comparing the purchase price of key materials from the major suppliers of Diggit.

Accounting system

Diggit uses a customised digital bookkeeping system. There is a rota system amongst you, Rosita and Morgan to do daily checks on the entries made. All bank receipts and payments and petty cash receipts and payments are entered manually into a cash book/petty cash book. The bank columns of the manual cash book are reconciled with the bank statement on a monthly basis. Maggie keeps the petty cash box on her desk and reimburses an expense when she receives a receipt.

All journals are recorded in a journal daybook.

Once a transaction is entered into the digital bookkeeping system, the system will automatically post entries to all relevant accounts. When a journal to write off an irrecoverable debt is entered, the system will also make the necessary adjustment to that particular customer's account in the receivables ledger.

Transactions are entered into the digital bookkeeping system by selecting the menu options. Payments to credit suppliers and receipts from credit customers are recorded using the Credit suppliers and Credit customer's menu options. All other payments and receipts are recorded according to the payment method.

These are the menu options you may need to use today:

Main menu	Sub menu
Credit suppliers	Purchase invoices
	Purchase credit notes
	Payments to credit suppliers
Credit customers	Sales invoices
	Sales credit notes
	Receipts from credit customers
Bank	Payments
	Receipts
Cash	Payments
	Receipts
Petty cash	Payments
	Receipts
General ledger	Journal entries

AAT: L2 END POINT ASSESSMENT

These are the accounting codes you may need to use today:

General ledger code	Account	General ledger code	Account
001	Sales – garden	601	Rent paid
002	Sales – barbecue	602	Repairs and maintenance
003	Sales – family events	603	Gas expense
004	Discounts allowed	604	Electricity expense
005	Purchases	605	Telephone expense
006	Discounts received	606	Motor expenses
101	Bank	607	Water rates
102	Cash in hand	608	Accountancy fees
103	Petty cash	609	Legal fees
201	Factory wages	610	Sundry expenses
202	Office wages	611	Insurance
203	Other salaries	612	Subsistence
204	HMRC liability	613	Bank charges and interest
205	Pension liability	614	Irrecoverable debts written off
402	Receivables ledger control	701	Capital
403	VAT control	702	Drawings
404	Payables ledger control	801	Suspense
405	Loan liability		
501	Land and buildings		
502	Motor vehicles		
503	Fixtures and fittings		
504	Plant and machinery		

Payroll information

The payroll details for the sales staff are as follows:

Name of employee	Employee code	Monthly salary	Commission percentage
Ezekiel Monroe	1632	£2,600.00	10%
Siddiq Janus	1674	£2,000.00	25%
Pamela Mercer	1823	£1,800.00	20%
Enid Anderson	1934	£1,650.00	30%
Leah Hornsby	1999	£1,480.00	24%

PRACTICE QUESTIONS: SECTION 1

Other information

Rick is keen to expand the business by winning more contracts with garden centres. To do this, he will need to open a second factory and significantly expand production.

During your recent appraisal you expressed a keen interest in the payroll function of the business. Maggie agreed that as part of your professional development, she would delegate the task of checking the payroll to you.

Diggit requires all accounting staff to have up-to-date knowledge in the areas of accounting systems and processes, bookkeeping controls and recognising and rectifying errors.

Staff must periodically complete a test comprising 13 questions to evidence their continuing professional development in these areas. You have been asked to complete the test today.

TASK 1

(a) Which of the following documents is sent from a purchaser to a supplier?

Document	
Credit note	
Purchase order	
Sales invoice	
Delivery note	

(b) If Diggit sells an item of machinery for £2,700 inclusive of VAT at 20%, what is the VAT amount in relation to this transaction?

VAT amount £	
£450 receivable from HMRC	
£540 payable to HMRC	
£540 receivable from HMRC	
£450 payable to HMRC	

(c) Which of the following will increase the capital of Diggit?

Transaction	
Payments for heating bills in the office	
Acquisition of a new piece of machinery for the office	
A loan taken out with the bank	
Money put in to the business by Rick Greene	

(d) Diggit issues suppliers with a unique code made up of a combination of the first few letters of their name, plus numerical values.

What type of code is this?

Type of code	
Sequential	
Faceted	
Block	
Alphanumeric	

TASK 2

(a) Which day book would credit notes RECEIVED from a supplier be recorded in?

Day book	
Sales returns day book	
Sales day book	
Purchases returns day book	
Purchases day book	

(b) Which of the following is true regarding a statement of profit or loss?

Statement	
It lists the money put into the company by the owner	
It contains all of the assets of the company	
It lists the amounts taken out of the company by the owner	
It contains the income and expenses of the company	

(c) What is the purpose of a sales credit note?

Purpose	
To reflect a discount that has been given	
To reflect that all or part of a previous sale has been cancelled	
To reflect that all or part of a previous purchase has been cancelled	
To record a credit sale	

(d) Which of the following principles explain why the statement of financial position balances?

Principle	
Separate entity principle	
Prudence principle	
Business principle	
Dual effect principle	

TASK 3

(a) Which of the following represents a DEBIT balance?

Balance	
Sales	
Purchases	
Payables ledger control account	
Capital introduced by the owner	

(b) A bank reconciliation reconciles the bank statement to what item?

Item	
Supplier statements	
Bank letter	
Cash book	
Customer statements	

(c) If Diggit gives a discount to a customer, which day book will it be recorded in?

Day book	
Discounts allowed day book	
Sales day book	
Sales returns day book	
Discounts received day book	

(d) A purchase of £400 exclusive of VAT at 20% was made by Diggit. Diggit will receive a 5% discount if they pay promptly.

If Diggit takes the prompt payment discount, how much will they pay?

Amount	
£380	
£456	
£460	
£480	

TASK 4

(a) Which of the following would not be included in the total wages expense for Diggit?

Wages expense	
Employer's pension contributions	
Employee's NIC contributions	
Employer's NIC contributions	
Gross wages	

(b) Jake Strong worked 20 hours this week in the factory. Jake also worked 5 hours driving at a family event on a national holiday.

What is Jake's gross wages for the week?

Gross wages	
£291	
£270	
£200	
£265	

(c) Which of the following items are credited to the wages control account?

Balance	
Total pension contributions	
Total wages expense	
Total HMRC liability	
Net wages paid	

(d) Pamela Mercer earned her normal salary plus £1,000 commission. Her PAYE for the month was £600. The employer's NIC and pension totalled £650 and the employee's NIC and pension contributions totalled £420.

What is Pamela's net pay for the month?

Net pay	
£1,130	
£2,780	
£1,780	
£1,550	

TASK 5

(a) Diggit makes a regular monthly payment of £12,500 to rent the warehouse.

What type of payment is this?

Payment type	
Direct debit	
BACS	
Faster Payment	
Standing order	

(b) Diggit paid an invoice in full to one of its suppliers. The goods had a list price of £6,000 excluding VAT at 20%, and Diggit received a trade discount of 3%.

What is the total credit to the bank for Diggit in respect of this transaction?

£	
6,984	
7,020	
6,000	
5,820	

(c) Diggit's bank balance showed a positive balance of £2,600. Rosita has paid in £1,000 to the bank from cash sales which have not yet cleared. Morgan has written cheques totalling £730 which are yet to be presented.

What will the balance on Diggit's cash book be?

£	
3,600	
2,870	
2,330	
1,870	

(d) Which of the following is a drawback of a digital bookkeeping system?

Purpose	
It cannot do calculations quickly	
It often makes tasks slower	
It can make reports more difficult to generate	
It can be costly to implement	

TASK 6

As the finance team has grown Maggie Grimes has been very keen to implement bookkeeping controls, particularly in the sales department.

(a) Identify TWO internal controls already in place in the sales department at Diggit.

Maggie would like to introduce more controls over the sales system, particularly in relation to the receivables as she is concerned about irrecoverable debts. Maggie is particularly worried that the commission system incentivises staff to pursue new customers rather than just growing sales.

(b) Identify THREE internal controls that could be introduced to help manage the receivables system.

AAT: L2 END POINT ASSESSMENT

TASK 7

Rosita keeps hearing people talking about management accounting and financial accounting but is unsure of the difference.

(a) Identify which of the statements below describes financial accounting.

Statement	
Financial accounting is for management usage and can be prepared on a regular basis	
Financial accounting is for external users and is generally prepared on an annual basis	
Financial accounting is generally less accurate than management accounting	
Financial accounting relates to the information provided solely to HMRC for tax calculations	

(b) Identify THREE reports run in Diggit that would be classed as management accounting reports.

(c) State ONE example of how Maggie could use the information gained from the monthly report run by the purchasing team.

TASK 8

Diggit classifies costs in different ways.

(a) Explain what is meant by a direct cost.

(b) Identify two direct costs incurred by Diggit.

(c) Rosita has heard Maggie say that the electricity costs are a semi-variable costs but is unsure what that means.

Explain to Rosita what a semi-variable cost is and why electricity is likely to be one.

AAT: L2 END POINT ASSESSMENT

TASK 9

You have been supplied with the following figures for the monthly wage bill of the factory:

Item	£
Gross wages	15,200
Employer's NIC	2,800
Employee's NIC	1,200
PAYE	3,750

(a) Write up the wages control account below, showing the net wages paid.

Wages control account

Item	Amount £	Item	Amount £

Picklist: Gross wages, Employer's NIC, Employee's NIC, PAYE, Net pay

You have also been informed of a late starter in the factory. Their timesheet shows they worked 20 hours this week and have already been paid through the bank. You need to make a late journal entry to ensure their wages are included in the digital bookkeeping system.

(b) Write up the wages control account below, showing the net wages paid.

Enter the wages into the digital bookkeeping system by:

— selecting the appropriate menu option

— completing the journal

Menu option:

[   ]

Picklist: Bank – Payments, Cash – Payments, Petty Cash – Payments,
General ledger – journal entries

General ledger code	Debit £	Credit £
Details: Journal to include the wages		

TASK 10

Morgan has informed you that a customer owing £600 inclusive of VAT at 20% has been declared bankrupt.

(a) Complete the journal below to record the entries in relation to this.

General ledger code	Debit £	Credit £
Details: Journal to write off the customer balance		

Picklist: 614, 610, 402, 403, 001, 101

You have been given the remittance below regarding the payment of some invoices. These invoices were paid at a 5% discount to the initial amount due to the customer taking a prompt payment discount.

Hilltop Ltd

VAT registration 446 1552 01

Remittance no: 384

To: Diggit   28 September 20XX

	£
Invoices 43241-43246	3,230
Amount net of 5% prompt payment discount	

(b) Enter the payment into the digital bookkeeping system by:

— selecting the appropriate menu option

— entering the details of the payment

Menu option:

Picklist: Credit suppliers – purchase invoices, Credit suppliers – purchase credit notes, Credit suppliers – payments to credit suppliers, Credit customers – sales invoices, Credit customers – sales credit notes, Credit customers – receipts from credit customers

Customer	Payment date	Invoice amount	Discount allowed	Payment amount
Hilltop	28 September			

TASK 11

Having made several entries into the digital bookkeeping system, you are checking your work when you notice some errors.

Firstly, you note that a payment for water rates of £600 was correctly credited to the bank but incorrectly credited to the water rates account.

(a) Select the correct general ledger codes and prepare entries in the journal daybook to:

- reverse the initial entry
- record the correct entries

Journal daybook

General ledger code	Debit £	Credit £
Details: Journal to reverse the initial entries		

Picklist: 101, 102, 103, 403, 605, 606, 607, 801

General ledger code	Debit £	Credit £
Details: Journal to record the correct entries		

Picklist: 101, 102, 103, 403, 605, 606, 607, 801

You have also been asked to check the work performed on the VAT control account.

(b) Identify whether the balances below should be shown as debits or credits in the VAT control account.

Item	Debit	Credit
VAT on purchases		
VAT on cash expenses		
VAT on sales		
VAT on sales returns		

PRACTICE QUESTIONS: SECTION 1

TASK 12

Morgan has started work on the monthly review of customer balances. He has sent you the note below, with the latest statement from a customer and an extract from the receivables ledger.

Note from Morgan:

> I was working through the control account reconciliation and noted some differences between the balances on a customer's statement and our receivables ledger. I have gone back to all of the original sales documentation and can confirm that all invoiced amounts are correct. It does appear that we have missed out some discounts correctly taken by the customer, and have not recorded a contra that we agreed to.
>
> Can you update our receivables ledger, confirm the correct balance and identify which items we need to report back to the customer on if they have any wrong?
>
> Thanks,
>
> Morgan

(a) Using the information from Morgan's note and the customer statement below, update the receivables ledger for the missing information.

Customer statement

Alexandria

To: Diggit   Account No: AL02

Statement of Account

Date 20XX	Detail	Payments £	Invoices £	Balance £
01 Sept	Balance b/d			1,000
01 Sept	Payment invoice 31456	950		50
01 Sept	Discount invoice 31456	50		0
01 Sept	Invoice 31489		1,580	1,580
11 Sept	Invoice 31523		2,450	4,030
12 Sept	Invoice 31527		2,380	6,410
13 Sept	Payment invoice 31489	1,500		4,910
15 Sept	Discount invoice 31489	80		4,830
17 Sept	Contra	600		4,230

KAPLAN PUBLISHING

Receivables ledger

Item	Amount £	Item	Amount £
Balance b/d	1,000	Payment received	950
Invoice 31489	1,580	Payment received	1,500
Invoice 31523	2,540		
Invoice 31527	2,830		

(b) What will be the balance carried down in the receivables ledger?

Amount	Debit/Credit

Picklist: Debit, Credit

You also need to provide the customer with the errors in their statement.

(c) Complete the statement below:

	£
Balance as per customer ledger	4,230
Invoice number	**Error amount**
Correct balance	

(d) What type of error has been made by the customer?

Error type	
Error of commission	
Transposition error	
Error of principle	
Error of omission	

TASK 13

Maggie has given you the following information relating to the future plans for Diggit.

Hi Michonne,

We have invested in some new machinery for the factory, and I think I'm right in saying that it is not an expense for the business? Can you process the entries for it please? The machinery cost £10,000 and we have been given 30 days to pay.

Also, we've just repaid £2,000 of our outstanding loan, but no entries have been made in the accounting records. Could you process this as well?

Maggie

(a) Prepare entries in the journal daybook to record the

- purchase of machinery
- repayment of loan

Journal daybook

Account name	Debit £	Credit £
Details: Journal to record the purchase of the machinery		

Picklist: Bank, Payables ledger control account, Plant and machinery, Loan liability, Capital

Account name	Debit £	Credit £
Details: Journal to record the repayment of the loan		

Picklist: Bank, Payables ledger control account, Plant and machinery, Loan liability, Capital

Rosita would like to know how certain items affect the accounting equation.

(b) How would a cash receipt from a credit customer affect the total assets?

Effect on assets	
Increase	
Decrease	
No effect	

Rick has taken an old delivery vehicle and some money from the bank for his own personal use.

(c) State whether the transaction above would result in a debit or credit to each item.

Item	Debit	Credit
Motor vehicles		
Drawings		
Bank		

AAT: L2 END POINT ASSESSMENT

SCENARIO 3

Blue BBQ

41 Kansas Way

Bluegrass

BG3 4RT

VAT registration 978 13521 93

Background information

Blue BBQ is owned by Ron Knope, a sole trader. The business sells a range of barbecue and hot sauces to the major supermarkets in its country. In addition, Blue BBQ designs custom sauces for sale to restaurants and sells some sauces in a factory shop.

The range of barbecue sauces and hot sauces are produced quickly and easily, with bottles always being completed at the end of a day's work in the factory. The customised products often take longer and a batch can take a number of days to complete.

The sauces are produced in a rented local factory before being transported to the warehouse at Blue BBQ's headquarters, where there is an office on-site where all the administration and distribution is managed.

The office and warehouse are owned by Blue BBQ, but the factory is rented under a short-term lease of 12 months with the annual rental charge agreed each year. The rental charge does not include any utility bills for the factory, merely the use of the premises and any equipment. It does include repairs to the factory equipment.

The factory manager and office staff are paid an annual fixed amount. The factory workers are paid an hourly rate and generally work 35 hours each week (7 hours a day), although overtime can be worked if approved by the factory manager.

The majority of the sales staff in the office receive a set wage plus commission for any new restaurant orders they have generated.

You are Leslie Swanson and work for Blue BBQ as a Finance Assistant. Today's date is 1 May 20XX. Your team consists of you and two other Finance Assistants called Anne Dwyer and Chris Perkins and you all report to your line manager, April Wyatt.

Any new suppliers must be requested by the purchasing department and approved by April Wyatt or Ron Knope. No order above £1,000 can be placed with a new supplier until they have successfully delivered five orders on time and of appropriate quality. April updates the system weekly to record any changes in the price of goods from suppliers. Finally, April sets automated payments to be made to suppliers just before any prompt payment discounts expire from each supplier.

Reports

April's team is responsible for preparing many reports for Blue BBQ. They have to prepare the statement of financial position and statement of profit or loss annually, and other internal reports as requested by Ron. These other reports have included items such as a comparison of units produced in the factory, reports of sales orders per product, and regular reports showing the wastage of ingredients. Some of these reports are requested on a weekly basis, others on a monthly basis.

PRACTICE QUESTIONS: SECTION 1

In addition to this, April's team are also responsible for producing reports which compare actual results to budgeted results each week, showing any adverse or favourable variances for Ron to investigate further.

VAT

The organisation operates the standard VAT scheme and VAT on all sales is at 20%.

Accounting system

Blue BBQ uses a customised digital bookkeeping system. There is a rota system amongst you, Anne and Chris to do daily checks on the entries made.

All journals are recorded in a journal daybook.

Once a transaction is entered into the digital bookkeeping system, the system will automatically post entries to all relevant accounts. When a journal to write off an irrecoverable debt is entered, the system will also make the necessary adjustment to that particular customer's account in the receivables ledger.

Transactions are entered into the digital bookkeeping system by selecting the menu options. Payments to credit suppliers and receipts from credit customers are recorded using the Credit suppliers and Credit customer's menu options. All other payments and receipts are recorded according to the payment method.

These are the menu options you may need to use today:

Main menu	Sub menu
Credit suppliers	Purchase invoices
	Purchase credit notes
	Payments to credit suppliers
Credit customers	Sales invoices
	Sales credit notes
	Receipts from credit customers
Bank	Payments
	Receipts
Cash	Payments
	Receipts
Petty cash	Payments
	Receipts
General ledger	Journal entries

KAPLAN PUBLISHING

These are the accounting codes you may need to use today:

General ledger code	Account	General ledger code	Account
001	Sales – supermarket	601	Rent paid
002	Sales – restaurant	602	Repairs and maintenance
003	Sales – factory shop	603	Gas expense
004	Discounts allowed	604	Electricity expense
005	Purchases	605	Telephone expense
006	Discounts received	606	Motor expenses
101	Bank	607	Water rates
102	Cash in hand	608	Accountancy fees
103	Petty cash	609	Legal fees
201	Factory wages	610	Sundry expenses
202	Office wages	611	Insurance
203	Other salaries	612	Subsistence
204	HMRC liability	613	Bank charges and interest
205	Pension liability	614	Irrecoverable debts written off
401	Wages control	701	Capital
402	Receivables ledger control	702	Drawings
403	VAT control	900	Suspense
404	Payables ledger control		
405	Bank loan		
501	Land and buildings		
502	Motor vehicles		
503	Fixtures and fittings		
504	Plant and machinery		

Payroll information

The payroll details for the sales staff are as follows:

Name of employee	Employee code	Monthly salary	Commission percentage
Ben Haverford	1132	£3,500.00	–%
Joan Ludgate	1374	£2,700.00	25%
Dennis Meagle	1423	£2,100.00	30%

PRACTICE QUESTIONS: SECTION 1

The payroll details for factory staff are as follows:

Employee grade	Hourly wage	Overtime rate
Factory supervisor	£17.30	£24.00
Senior factory employee	£15.00	£21.00
Junior factory employee	£12.50	£18.00

Other information

Ron is keen to expand the business by increasing orders with supermarkets. To do this, he will need to extend credit terms to major supermarkets in the country.

During your recent appraisal you expressed a keen interest in the payroll function of the business. April agreed that as part of your professional development, she would delegate the task of checking the payroll to you.

Blue BBQ requires all accounting staff to have up-to-date knowledge in the areas of accounting systems and processes, bookkeeping controls and recognising and rectifying errors.

Staff must periodically complete a test comprising 13 questions to evidence their continuing professional development in these areas. You have been asked to complete the test today.

TASK 1

(a) Which of the following is an expense for Blue BBQ?

Item	
Recording an irrecoverable debt	
New tablet computers for the sales staff	
Making a repayment of a loan owed	
Paying off an amount owed to a supplier	

(b) Which item is classified as an asset of Blue BBQ?

Item	
A bank overdraft	
The wages of the sales staff	
Money owed from credit customers	
Money taken out of the business by Ron for personal use	

(c) Which item would reduce the capital in Blue BBQ?

Item	
A sale of goods on credit	
Paying an amount owed to a supplier	
Acquisition of new machinery	
Purchase of stationery	

(d) Which two items are not classified as liabilities of Blue BBQ?

Item	
Cash paid to repaint the factory	
Purchase of goods on credit	
Output VAT on sales	
Money invested into the business by Ron	

TASK 2

(a) What is the name for a budget that remains the same regardless of volume?

Budget	
General budget	
Set budget	
Fixed budget	
Determined budget	

(b) If Blue BBQ's actual costs exceed their budgeted costs, what does this represent?

Description	
Favourable variance	
Cost allocation problem	
Variable budget	
Adverse variance	

(c) Anne has noted that direct material costs for the month were £46,300 and the budgeted costs were £48,100.

Calculate the percentage variance to two decimal places.

Variance	
1.80%	
3.74%	
3.89%	
0.00%	

(d) Blue BBQ hot sauce requires a blend of spices which cost £1.20 per bottle. It also requires 100 ml of vinegar. Blue BBQ acquires vinegar in 1 litre bottles which cost £1 each.

What is the budgeted material cost for 20 bottles of hot sauce?

Budgeted cost	
£23.20	
£24	
£44	
£26	

TASK 3

(a) Which of these items is a common reconciling item in a bank reconciliation?

Item	
Contras	
Unpresented cheques	✓
Transposition errors	
Goods in transit at year-end	

(b) A list of balances owed by individual customers is known by what name?

Name	
Receivables ledger control account	
Customer account list	
Sales account reconciliation	
Receivables ledger	✓

(c) When is a contra made?

Contra	
Where a company is both a customer and supplier	✓
Where a customer takes a discount	
When a supplier gives a discount	
Where a customer is declared bankrupt	

(d) Which of the following would be a debit to the receivables ledger control account?

Transaction	
New cash sales	
Payment received from a credit customer	
New credit sales	✓
Discounts given to customers	

TASK 4

(a) Which of the workers in Blue BBQ are not salaried staff?

Staff	
Factory manager	
Office staff	
Sales staff	
Factory workers	

(b) Blue BBQ is considering moving to output related pay in the factory.

Which of the following could be a disadvantage of doing this?

Disadvantage	
There is an inconsistent labour cost per unit	
Employees have no incentive to produce more units	
Quality could diminish if workers rush to make more units	
It discourages efficient work, disincentivising workers	

(c) One of the factory teams consists of a supervisor, 2 senior factory staff and 10 junior staff.

In a typical 7-hour working day, what is the cost to Blue BBQ of the team?

Cost	
£313.60	
£1,206.10	
£1,101.10	
£1,085.00	

(d) If Joan Ludgate generates new orders totalling £2,000, Ben Haverford generates no new orders and Dennis Meagle generates new orders totalling £3,000, which member of the sales team will earn the most in a month?

Employee	
Ben Haverford	
Joan Ludgate	
Dennis Meagle	
All earn the same	

TASK 5

(a) Anne has asked you some questions about VAT.

Which of the following statements regarding VAT is true?

Statement	
VAT is deducted from the net sales price when recording revenue in the financial statements	
VAT on the sales of sauce can be reclaimed from HMRC	
VAT can be reclaimed on an irrecoverable debt	
VAT is owed to HMRC on expenses paid by Blue BBQ	

(b) Which of the following has no impact on the amount of VAT to be paid?

Transaction	
Trade discounts given to customers	
Prompt payment discount taken by customers	
Bulk discounts given on large sales	
All these transactions impact the amount of VAT to be paid	

(c) Blue BBQ buys bottles totalling £430 inclusive of VAT at 20%.

What amount and type of VAT is this?

Amount and type	
£71.67 output VAT	
£71.67 input VAT	
£86 output VAT	
£86 input VAT	

(d) A sales invoice for a credit customer has been entered as a sales credit note incorrectly in the digital bookkeeping system.

Identify the consequence of this error.

Consequence	
The total sales value will be understated	
The business may despatch goods that have not been sold	
The total amount owed to payables will be understated	
The business may be paid for goods that have not been sold	

TASK 6

You have spoken to April about controls, and she is very proud about the controls that Blue BBQ has over the purchases system.

(a) Identify THREE internal controls already in place in the purchases system at Blue BBQ.

(b) Identify TWO potential problems that Blue BBQ will avoid by having the controls in place over the purchases system.

AAT: L2 END POINT ASSESSMENT

TASK 7

Chris is unsure of the difference between financial accounting reports and management accounting reports.

(a) Identify one report prepared by April's team that will be a financial accounting report and one which will be a management accounting report.

(b) Using the example of the reports produced by April's team, outline THREE differences between management accounting and financial accounting reports. This can be in terms of their preparation, their content, their layout, or how they are used.

TASK 8

Chris has heard of FIFO and LIFO for valuing inventory, but has been told there is another method.

(a) What is the name of this other method and how is it calculated?

Chris is still unsure of how the methods work and has been reading about inflation.

(b) In times of inflation, describe which method would give the HIGHEST valuation for inventory and why.

(c) Identify ONE potential item of work-in-progress that could exist at the end of a week in Blue BBQ.

AAT: L2 END POINT ASSESSMENT

TASK 9

Anne has received the following information regarding two employees. Jerry Trager is a senior full-time factory employee and Dennis Girgich is a junior factory employee who works four days a week.

Anne has also received confirmation that overtime has been approved in relation to senior employees and is therefore valid. No overtime was approved for junior employees.

Employee Name: Jerry Trager   Employee Code: 915
Timesheet number: 1167

Date	Day of week	Total hours
11.09.20XX	Monday to Friday	41
16.09.20XX	Saturday	6
		47

Employee Name: Dennis Girgich   Employee Code: 946
Timesheet number: 1173

Date	Day of week	Total hours
11.09.20XX	Monday to Thursday	28

(a) Enter the timesheets into the digital bookkeeping system by entering the details of the timesheet.

Employee code	Timesheet number	Number of hours	Rate £	Rate per hour £
915	1167			
915	1167			

Picklist: Normal rate, Overtime rate

Employee code	Timesheet number	Number of hours	Rate £	Rate per hour £
946	1173			

Picklist: Normal rate, Overtime rate

50   KAPLAN PUBLISHING

PRACTICE QUESTIONS: SECTION 1

You have been supplied with the following figures as the monthly wage bill for the factory:

Item	£
Gross wages	40,000
Employer's NIC	5,200
Employee's NIC	3,800
PAYE	11,300
Employer pension	3,200
Employee pension	1,900

(b) Show how the wages expense will be recorded in the general ledger.

Account name	Amount £	Debit	Credit

Picklist: 201, 202, 203, 401

TASK 10

You have been given the credit note below from a member of the team in relation to a complaint from a customer who received some sauce bottles that had passed their best-before date. This relates to the gross amount invoiced to the customer, who has informed Blue BBQ that they will not be paying any of it.

Blue BBQ

VAT registration 978 13521 93

Credit note number 163

To: JWM Supermarkets   28 September 20XX

                                                                          £

450 of product code 425 @ £2.00 each   900

(a) Enter the credit note into the digital bookkeeping system by:

- selecting the appropriate menu option
- entering the details of the credit note

Menu option:

Picklist: Credit suppliers – purchase invoices, Credit suppliers – purchase credit notes, Credit suppliers – payments to credit suppliers, Credit customers – sales invoices, Credit customers – sales credit notes, Credit customers – receipts from credit customers

Customer	Invoice date	Invoice number	Net amount £	VAT £	Total amount £
JWM	28 September	CN163			

(b) Select the correct general ledger codes and show the entries required to record the credit note.

General ledger code	Debit £	Credit £

Picklist: 001, 002, 003, 402, 403, 610, 614

TASK 11

Having made several entries into the digital bookkeeping system you are checking your work when you notice an error. A bank payment for electricity costs of £500 was incorrectly recorded as a credit in the electricity account. The bank entry was recorded correctly and a suspense account was created in order to make the ledgers balance.

(a) Select the correct general ledger codes and prepare entries in the journal daybook to:

- remove the original entries
- record the correct entries

Journal daybook

General ledger code (picklist)	Debit £	Credit £
Details: journal to remove the original entries		

Picklist: 604, 610, 503, 101, 102, 900

General ledger code (picklist)	Debit £	Credit £
Details: journal to record the correct entries		

Picklist: 604, 610, 503, 101, 102, 900

(b) Identify whether the errors below will lead to the creation of a suspense account or not.

Error	Will create a suspense account	No suspense account created
A purchase of machinery was incorrectly debited to repairs and maintenance expense.		
Chris has forgotten to record a journal for an irrecoverable debt.		
A petty cash payment of £30 was credited to cash with no other entry made.		
A credit sale of £1,000 was debited to sales and credited to the receivables ledger control account.		

AAT: L2 END POINT ASSESSMENT

TASK 12

Anne has started work on the monthly review of supplier balances. She has sent you the note below, with the latest statement from a supplier and an extract from the payables ledger.

> I was working through the control account reconciliation and noted some differences between the balances on a supplier's statement and our payables ledger. I have gone back to all of the original purchases documentation and can confirm that all of the invoiced amounts on the customer statement are correct. It does appear that we have incorrectly taken some discounts, have recorded a contra against the wrong customer. However, the supplier statement is missing some goods which we returned due to being poor quality.
>
> Can you update our payables ledger, confirm the correct balance and identify which items we need to report back to the supplier if they have any wrong?
>
> Thanks,
>
> Anne

Supplier statement

Poorknee Ltd

To: Blue BBQ   Account No: PK01

Statement of Account

Date 20XX	Detail	Payments £	Invoices £	Balance £
01 Sept	Balance b/d			2,000
01 Sept	Payment invoice 31456	100		1,900
01 Sept	Invoice 24344		1,200	3,100
01 Sept	Invoice 24345		1,450	4,550
11 Sept	Invoice 24346		2,000	6,550
12 Sept	Invoice 24347		3,200	9,750
13 Sept	Payment invoice 24344	1,200		8,550
15 Sept	Payment invoice 24345	1,450		7,100

Payables ledger

Item	Amount £	Item	Amount £
Payment made	1,200	Balance b/d	1,900
Payment made	1,450	Invoice 24344	1,200
Contra	600	Invoice 24345	1,450
Goods returned	700	Invoice 24346	1,800
		Invoice 24347	2,900

PRACTICE QUESTIONS: **SECTION 1**

(a) Using the information from Anne's note and the supplier statement above, note the corrections which must be made to the payables ledger.

Error	Amount to adjust £	Debit/Credit
Invoice 24346		
Invoice 24347		
Contra		

Picklist: Debit, Credit

(b) What will be the balance carried down in the payables ledger?

Amount £	Debit/Credit

Picklist: Debit, Credit

You need to provide the supplier with the errors in their statement. Complete the table below.

(c) Complete the statement below:

	£
Balance as per supplier statement	7,100
Item	Error amount
Correct balance	

(d) What type of error has been made?

Error type	
Error of commission	
Transposition error	
Error of principle	
Error of omission	

KAPLAN PUBLISHING

AAT: L2 END POINT ASSESSMENT

TASK 13

April has forwarded you the following message from Ron:

> Hi April,
>
> We are looking to expand our sales to national supermarkets and we are therefore going to be opening a new distribution facility in order to meet that demand. The distribution facility is going to cost approximately £200,000.
>
> To fund this, we have received a bank loan of £150,000 and I will have also transferred £50,000 of my own money into Blue BBQ.
>
> Can you make the journal entries to record these transactions in the ledgers please?
>
> Thanks,
>
> Ron

(a) Prepare entries in the journal daybook to record the

- bank loan
- money from Ron

Journal daybook

Account code	Debit £	Credit £
Details: Journal to record the bank loan		

Picklist: 101, 103, 404, 405, 501, 701, 702

Account code	Debit £	Credit £
Details: Journal to record the deposit of money from Ron		

Picklist: 101, 103, 404, 405, 501, 701, 702

Anne would like to know why the money from Ron is recorded in a different place to the money from the bank.

(b) Which of the following principles will you use to explain this to Anne?

Accounting principle	
Accounting equation	
Business entity	
Dual aspect	

(c) Using the information from the list below, total the amounts to be recorded in assets, liabilities and expenses.

Item	Amount £
Owned distribution facility	200,000
Purchases	24,500
Bank account (overdrawn)	1,500
Payables ledger control	10,000
Discounts allowed	2,400
Receivables ledger control	16,600

Assets £	Liabilities £	Expenses £

Section 2

ANSWERS TO PRACTICE QUESTIONS

SCENARIO 1

TASK 1

(a) Which of the following is not a routine task?

Tasks	
Checking all orders have been delivered	
Checking the condition of goods sent to a customer	
Sending sales invoices when goods are delivered	
Performing an analysis of whether any companies are breaching their payment terms	✓

(b) Which item is classified as a non-current asset of Keep it Clean?

Item	
Factory owned by Keep it Clean	✓
Delivery vehicles rented by Keep it Clean	
Keep it Clean's bank account	
Inventory of clothing for sale	

(c) Which item is classified as an expense of Keep it Clean?

Item	
A debt written off in relation to a customer	✓
Drawings by the owner of the business	
Cash put into the business by the owner	
Items returned by a customer	

(d) If Keep It Clean always tops up petty cash to the same amount, what is the name of this system?

System	
Voucher system	
Constant float method	
Imprest system	✓
Reimbursement method	

KAPLAN PUBLISHING

TASK 2

(a) Which of these documents would be issued by Keep it Clean to a customer who has returned clothes due to poor quality?

Document	
Sales invoice	
Credit note	✓
Debit note	
Remittance advice	

(b) Each customer of Keep it Clean is given a code made up of numbers, with the number increasing each time a new customer is registered. What type of code is this?

Type of code	
Alphanumeric	
Faceted	
Sequential	✓
Alphabetical	

(c) Which of the following benefits is true in respect of a coding system?

Benefits of coding system	
It reduces the time taken to find transactions	
It helps categorise items by class	
It can help to reduce errors	
All of the above	✓

(d) What document is often sent with a customer's payment to inform the company which items are being paid?

Document	
Debit note	
Payment slip	
Quotation	
Remittance advice	✓

ANSWERS TO PRACTICE QUESTIONS: SECTION 2

TASK 3

(a) Which of the following accounts would not be affected by a credit sale of adult's clothes?

Account	
Cash	✓
Sales	
VAT	
Trade receivables	

The accounting entry for a credit sale is debit trade receivables, credit VAT, credit sales.

(b) If a customer with an outstanding balance relating to adult clothes is declared bankrupt, which of the following accounts would not be affected in recording this?

Account	
614 Irrecoverable debts written off	
402 Receivables ledger control	
001 Sale – adult clothes	✓
403 VAT control	

The sale occurred however the debt is now irrecoverable.

(c) When a credit customer makes a payment for an outstanding balance owed in respect of children's clothes, taking advantage of an early payment discount, which of the following isn't recorded in the entries?

Entries	
Deduct from receivables	
Include in cash	
Include in sales	✓
Record a discount allowed	

A credit customer taking advantage of an early payment discount would reduce the receivables balance (for both the cash received and the discount allowed), the cash receipt for the amount owed would be recorded as received in cash and the discount allowed would be recorded as an expense.

(d) Which of the following would not be a reason for the difference between the balance on the receivables ledger control account and the total of the receivables ledger balances?

Reason	
Discounts allowed were recorded in the ledger balances but not the control account	
A late sale was only recorded in the control account	
A sale of £630 was recorded as £360 in both the control account and ledger accounts	✓
Payments received were recorded at £410 in the control account and £400 in the receivables ledger balances	

KAPLAN PUBLISHING   61

TASK 4

(a) In addition to gross wages, which of the items below would be included in Keep it Clean's wages expense?

Wages expense	
Employee charitable deductions	
PAYE deductions	
Employer's NIC	✓
Employee's NIC	

(b) Which of these items would explain why an employee's net pay is different to their gross pay?

Item	
Bonus payments	
Paid annual leave	
Overtime payments	
PAYE deductions	✓

(c) If Gigi prepares the payroll calculations and authorises the payroll, what risk does this process present?

Issue	
Risk of fraud due to lack of segregation of duties	✓
It is illegal for Gigi to do if she is not a qualified accountant	
Payroll should be done by someone more senior than Gigi	
Payroll must be done by external people, not employees	

(d) What is Nish's net pay this month?

Amount	
£2,381	
£2,893	✓
£3,405	
£1,393	

TASK 5

(a) Which of the following correctly shows the gross amount on the invoice?

Amount	
£1,440	
£1,380	
£1,428	
£1,368	✓

100 × £12 × 120% × 95% = £1,368

ANSWERS TO PRACTICE QUESTIONS: **SECTION 2**

(b) What is the amount that Keep it Clean can record in sales in respect of this transaction?

Amount	
£1,344	
£2,016	
£1,400	✓
£1,680	

£1,680 × 100/120 = £1,400

(c) What is the correct double entry to record this payment?

Entry	
Dr Bank, Cr VAT	
Dr VAT, Cr Bank	✓
Dr Sales, Cr VAT	
Dr VAT, Cr Sales	

(d) Which of the following is considered a feature of a digital bookkeeping system?

Transaction	
It is a backup of physical records	
It doesn't require a password to access the system	
It is a system which stores accounting records online	✓
It removes the need for bank payments to be authorised	

TASK 6

(a) Identify TWO internal controls already in place in respect of payroll at Keep it Clean.

> Overtime is only paid if it can be supported by approval from the factory manager.
>
> Commission is only paid if it agrees to the documentation from the sales manager.

(b) Identify THREE internal controls that could be introduced to help improve the payroll system.

> Have a separate member of the payroll team prepare the payroll and have Gigi Osborne review and authorise it.
>
> Ensure all new starter information is received for new factory staff before paying them.
>
> Review the dates worked by events staff and compare to a national holiday calendar and a list of the ethical fashion events attended by Keep it Clean.
>
> Ensure event staff hours are approved by a relevant manager, possibly the sales manager.

TASK 7

(a) Identify which report from Gigi is not classified as a management accounting report.

> The statement of profit or loss.

(b) Identify THREE other major elements of non-payroll costs that would be incurred by Keep it Clean and could be included in a budget of total company expenses.

> Energy costs in the factory
>
> Office running costs
>
> Rental costs for the vehicles
>
> Purchase costs of raw materials
>
> Delivery costs to the major customers
>
> Discounts given to major customers
>
> Irrecoverable debts.
>
> **Note:** Other relevant answers can be accepted.

(c) State ONE example of how the Finance Director may use the information in Gigi's report of returns to each supplier.

> Could identify poor performing suppliers and limit the purchases to be made from these.
>
> Perform a subsequent check to ensure a credit note received from supplier.

TASK 8

(a) Explain what is meant by an indirect cost.

> Indirect costs apply to more than one business activity and can't be associated with one specific item of production.

(b) Identify one fixed cost incurred by Keep it Clean.

> Office salaries
>
> Rent of delivery vehicles.

(c) State TWO costs incurred by Keep it Clean which are indirect costs.

> Power costs in the factory
>
> Labour costs in the factory
>
> Selling or marketing costs
>
> Administrative salaries
>
> General administration costs.

ANSWERS TO PRACTICE QUESTIONS: SECTION 2

TASK 9

(a) Enter the timesheet into the digital bookkeeping system by:

– selecting the appropriate menu option

– entering the details of the timesheet

Menu option

General ledger – journal entries

Employee code	Timesheet number	Number of hours	Rate	Rate per hour
2293	1167	14.5	Normal	15.20
2293	1167	8	Overtime	21.28

£15.20 × 140% = £21.28

(b) Show how the wages expense will be recorded in the general ledger

Account name	Amount £	Debit	Credit
Wages expense	53,210	✓	
Wages control	53,210		✓

Wages expense = £45,000 + £5,610 + £2,600 = £53,210

TASK 10

(a) Complete the entries below by inserting:

– the monthly salary for each individual

– the amount of commission each staff member should receive

Sales staff commission schedule

Employee	Employee code	Salary £	Commission £
James Gamble	2342	2,100	352
Jessica Horne	2858	1,280	414

22% × £1,600 = £352, 18% × £2,300 = £414

(b) Record the double entry required to account for the purchase return.

Debit/credit	Account (Picklist)	Amount £
Dr	Trade payables	540
Cr	VAT	90
Cr	Purchase returns	450

TASK 11

(a) What will be the balance brought down in the payables ledger control account after you have entered this transaction, and will it be a debit or credit?

Amount £	Debit/Credit
14,220	Credit

Picklist: Debit, Credit

(b) Select the correct general ledger codes and prepare entries in the journal daybook to:

– remove the incorrect entries

– record the correct entries

Journal daybook

General ledger code (picklist)	Debit £	Credit £
102	300	
005		250
403		50
Details: journal to remove the incorrect entries		

General ledger code (picklist)	Debit £	Credit £
102	300	
001		250
403		50
Details: journal to record the correct entries		

ANSWERS TO PRACTICE QUESTIONS: SECTION 2

TASK 12

(a) What will be the balance carried down in the cash book?

£	Debit/credit
12,040	Credit

Date 20XX	Details	Bank £	Date 20XX	Cheque number	Details	Bank £
01 Sept	Balance b/d	10,740	07 Sept	110157	Waterfall	390
1 Sept	Smith	180	07 Sept	110158	Crocombe	600
14 Sept	Event sales	850	07 Sept	110159	Efete	240
16 Sept	Maher	990	07 Sept	110160	Glennon	1,060
22 Sept	McAtee	500	07 Sept	110161	Amos	400
20 Sept	Holahan	1,030	23 Sept	DD	Electricity	300
22 Sept	Event sales	520				
01 Sept	Interest received	120				
23 Sept	Interest received	100				
			30 Sept		Balance c/d	**12,040**
		15,030				15,030

(b) Bank reconciliation statement as at 23 June 20XX

Balance per bank statement	11,650
Outstanding lodgements (name)	
McAtee	500
Holahan	1,030
Event sales	520
Unpresented cheques (number)	
110158	–600
110160	–1,060
Balance as per cash book	12,040

KAPLAN PUBLISHING

AAT: L2 END POINT ASSESSMENT

TASK 13

(a) Prepare entries in the journal daybook to record the injection of cash and advertising in the fashion magazine.

Journal daybook

Account name	Debit £	Credit £
101	30,000	
701		30,000
Details: Journal to record the cash injection		

Account name	Debit £	Credit £
610	5,000	
101		5,000
Details: Journal to record the advertisement		

Note: in the absence of a specific advertising or marketing account, this has been allocated to sundry expenses.

(b) Which of the following principles will you use to explain this to Emma?

Accounting principle	
Accounting equation	
Business entity	✓
Dual aspect	

(c) Using the information from the list below, total the amounts to be recorded in assets, liabilities and capital.

Item	Amount £
Owned equipment	18,000
Bank account	27,000
Loan owed to bank	13,000
Money injected by Charlene	30,000
Receivables ledger control	8,000

Assets £	Liabilities £	Capital £
53,000	13,000	30,000

Total assets = £18,000 + £27,000 + £8,000

The loan is a liability and the money injected by Charlene is held as capital.

ANSWERS TO PRACTICE QUESTIONS: SECTION 2

SCENARIO 2

TASK 1

(a) Which of the following documents is sent from a purchaser to a supplier?

Document	
Credit note	
Purchase order	✓
Sales invoice	
Delivery note	

(b) If Diggit sells an item of machinery for £2,700 inclusive of VAT at 20%, what is the VAT amount in relation to this transaction?

VAT amount £	
£450 receivable from HMRC	
£540 payable to HMRC	
£540 receivable from HMRC	
£450 payable to HMRC	✓

£2,700 × 20/120 = £450

(c) Which of the following will increase the capital of Diggit?

Transaction	
Payments for heating bills in the office	
Acquisition of a new piece of machinery for the office	
A loan taken out with the bank	
Money put in to the business by Rick Greene	✓

(d) What type of code is this?

Type of code	
Sequential	
Faceted	
Block	
Alphanumeric	✓

KAPLAN PUBLISHING

TASK 2

(a) Which day book would credit notes RECEIVED from a supplier be recorded in?

Day book	
Sales returns day book	
Sales day book	
Purchases returns day book	✓
Purchases day book	

(b) Which of the following is true regarding a statement of profit or loss?

Statement	
It lists the money put into the company by the owner	
It contains all of the assets of the company	
It lists the amounts taken out of the company by the owner	
It contains the income and expenses of the company	✓

(c) What is the purpose of a sales credit note?

Purpose	
To reflect a discount that has been given	
To reflect that all or part of a previous sale has been cancelled	✓
To reflect that all or part of a previous purchase has been cancelled	
To record a credit sale	

(d) Which of the following principles explain why the statement of financial position balances?

Principle	
Separate entity principle	
Prudence principle	
Business principle	
Dual effect principle	✓

ANSWERS TO PRACTICE QUESTIONS: SECTION 2

TASK 3

(a) Which of the following represents a DEBIT balance?

Balance	
Sales	
Purchases	✓
Payables ledger control account	
Capital introduced by the owner	

(b) A bank reconciliation reconciles the bank statement to what item?

Item	
Supplier statements	
Bank letter	
Cash book	✓
Customer statements	

(c) If Diggit gives a discount to a customer, which day book will it be recorded in?

Day book	
Discounts allowed day book	✓
Sales day book	
Sales returns day book	
Discounts received day book	

(d) If Diggit takes the prompt payment discount, how much will they pay?

Amount	
£380	
£456	✓
£460	
£480	

£400 × 120% × 95% = £456

KAPLAN PUBLISHING

TASK 4

(a) Which of the following would not be included in the total wages expense for Diggit?

Wages expense	
Employer's pension contributions	
Employee's NIC contributions	✓
Employer's NIC contributions	
Gross wages	

(b) What is Jake's gross wages for the week?

Gross wages	
£291	✓
£270	
£200	
£265	

Working: 20 hours × £10 = £200, plus 5 hours at £18.20 (£14 at 30% premium) = £291

(c) Which of the following items are credited to the wages control account?

Balance	
Total pension contributions	
Total wages expense	✓
Total HMRC liability	
Net wages paid	

(d) What is Pamela's net pay for the month?

Net pay	
£1,130	
£2,780	
£1,780	✓
£1,550	

£1,800 + £1,000 − £600 − £420 = £1,780

ANSWERS TO PRACTICE QUESTIONS: **SECTION 2**

TASK 5

(a) What type of payment is this?

Payment type	
Direct debit	
BACS	
Faster Payment	
Standing order	✓

(b) What is the total credit to the bank for Diggit in respect of this transaction?

£	
6,984	✓
7,020	
6,000	
5,820	

£6,000 × 120% × 97% = £6,984

(c) What will the balance on Diggit's cash book be?

£	
3,600	
2,870	✓
2,330	
1,870	

£2,600 + £1,000 − £730 = £2,870

(d) Which of the following is a drawback of a digital bookkeeping system?

Purpose	
It cannot do calculations quickly	
It often makes tasks slower	
It can make reports more difficult to generate	
It can be costly to implement	✓

KAPLAN PUBLISHING

AAT: L2 END POINT ASSESSMENT

TASK 6

(a) Identify TWO internal controls already in place in the sales department at Diggit.

> New customers have credit checks performed on them which is reviewed by the sales manager.
>
> New customers are given a sequential numbered code.
>
> Any sales made with commission are checked by the finance manager to ensure they are with new customers.

(b) Identify THREE internal controls that could be introduced to help manage the receivables system.

> Set lower credit limits for the new customers until they have built up a payment history.
>
> Ensure supplies are not sent to any customer whose balance is overdue for settlement.
>
> Perform a monthly check to compare customer balances to credit limits.
>
> Perform a monthly check to compare receivable balances to payment period to see if any debts are overdue.
>
> Set automated limits to ensure no customer can go over their credit limit.
>
> Change the commission system so it isn't simply targeted towards new customers.

TASK 7

(a) Identify which of the statements below describes financial accounting.

Statement	
Financial accounting is for management usage and can be prepared on a regular basis	
Financial accounting is for external users and is generally prepared on an annual basis	✓
Financial accounting is generally less accurate than management accounting	
Financial accounting relates to the information provided solely to HMRC for tax calculations	

ANSWERS TO PRACTICE QUESTIONS: SECTION 2

(b) Identify THREE reports run in Diggit that would be classed as management accounting reports.

> The sales manager submits a report to the Finance Director at the end of every month, with details of new orders generated by each member of the sales team.
>
> The factory manager produces a report of units produced per week.
>
> The factory manager produces a report on the amount of downtime in a week due to damaged machinery.
>
> The warehouse supervisor produces a report showing the outstanding orders not delivered at the end of each week.
>
> The purchasing team also runs a monthly report comparing the purchase price of key materials from the major suppliers of Diggit.
>
> Any 3 of these would be correct.

(c) State ONE example of how Maggie could use the information gained from the monthly report run by the purchasing team.

> The finance team could use this report to ensure that only the suppliers with the best prices are used.
>
> Alternatively, they could compare this report to another report recording issues with the quality of goods, in order to create a list of recommended suppliers.

TASK 8

(a) Explain what is meant by a direct cost.

> A direct cost is directly traceable to a cost unit.

(b) Identify two direct costs incurred by Diggit.

> Direct labour – the factory workers making the equipment.
>
> Direct materials – the raw materials that go into producing the equipment.
>
> The fuel cost incurred in delivering goods to the customers.
>
> The commission earned by sales staff for new contracts.

(c) Explain to Rosita what a semi-variable cost is and why electricity is likely to be one.

> A semi-variable cost has a fixed element and a variable element. This means that there will be a fixed amount regardless of use, plus a variable element that increases with usage. The electricity may have a fixed fee (known as a standing charge) for being provided, plus an additional rate per KwH of electricity used.

AAT: L2 END POINT ASSESSMENT

TASK 9

(a) Write up the wages control account below, showing the net wages paid.

Wages control account

Item	Amount £	Item	Amount £
Employee's NIC	1,200	Gross wages	15,200
PAYE	3,750	Employer's NIC	2,800
Net pay (balance)	13,050		
	18,000		18,000

(b) Write up the wages control account below, showing the net wages paid.

Enter the wages into the digital bookkeeping system by:

– selecting the appropriate menu option

– completing the journal

Menu option

General ledger – journal entries

General ledger code	Debit £	Credit £
201	200	
101		200
Details: Journal to include the wages		

20 hours ×£10 = £200

TASK 10

(a) Complete the journal below to record the entries in relation to this.

General ledger code	Debit £	Credit £
614	500	
403	100	
402		600
Details: Journal to write off the customer balance		

£500 ×20/120 = £100 VAT

ANSWERS TO PRACTICE QUESTIONS: SECTION 2

(b) Enter the payment into the digital bookkeeping system by:
- selecting the appropriate menu option
- entering the details of the payment

Menu option:

| Credit customers – receipts from credit customers |

Customer	Payment date	Invoice amount	Discount allowed	Payment amount
Hilltop	28 September	£3,400	£170	£3,230

£3,230 × 100/95 = £3,400

TASK 11

(a) Select the correct general ledger codes and prepare entries in the journal daybook to:
- reverse the initial entry
- record the correct entries

Journal daybook

General ledger code	Debit £	Credit £
101	600	
607	600	
801		1,200

Details: Journal to reverse the initial entries

General ledger code	Debit £	Credit £
101		600
607	600	

Details: Journal to record the correct entries

(b) Identify whether the balances below should be shown as debits or credits in the VAT control account.

Item	Debit	Credit
VAT on purchases	✓	
VAT on cash expenses	✓	
VAT on sales		✓
VAT on sales returns	✓	

TASK 12

(a) Using the information from Morgan's note and the customer statement below, update the receivables ledger for the missing information.

Receivables ledger

Item	Amount £	Item	Amount £
Balance b/d	1,000	Payment received	950
Invoice 31489	1,580	Payment received	1,500
Invoice 31523	2,540	Discount allowed	50
Invoice 31527	2,830	Discount allowed	80
		Contra	600
		Balance c/d	4,770
	7,950		7,950

(b) What will be the balance carried down in the receivables ledger?

Amount	Debit/Credit
£4,770	Credit

(c) Complete the statement below:

	£
Balance as per customer ledger	4,230
Invoice number	Error amount
31523	90
31527	450
Correct balance	4,770

(d) What type of error has been made by the customer?

Error type	
Error of commission	
Transposition error	✓
Error of principle	
Error of omission	

ANSWERS TO PRACTICE QUESTIONS: SECTION 2

TASK 13

(a) Prepare entries in the journal daybook to record the
- purchase of machinery
- repayment of loan

Journal daybook

Account name	Debit £	Credit £
Plant and machinery	10,000	
Payables ledger control account		10,000
Details: Journal to record the purchase of the machinery		

Account name	Debit £	Credit £
Loan liability	2,000	
Bank		2,000
Details: Journal to record the repayment of the loan		

(b) How would a cash receipt from a credit customer affect the total assets?

Effect on assets	
Increase	
Decrease	
No effect	✓

This would increase cash but reduce receivables resulting in no net effect on assets.

(c) State whether the transaction above would result in a debit or credit to each item.

Item	Debit	Credit
Motor vehicles		✓
Drawings	✓	
Bank		✓

SCENARIO 3

TASK 1

(a) Which of the following is an expense for Blue BBQ?

Item	
Recording an irrecoverable debt	✓
New tablet computers for the sales staff	
Making a repayment of a loan owed	
Paying off an amount owed to a supplier	

(b) Which item is classified as an asset of Blue BBQ?

Item	
A bank overdraft	
The wages of the sales staff	
Money owed from credit customers	✓
Money taken out of the business by Ron for personal use	

(c) Which item would reduce the capital in Blue BBQ?

Item	
A sale of goods on credit	
Paying an amount owed to a supplier	
Acquisition of new machinery	
Purchase of stationery	✓

The stationery is an expense, so would reduce profit and therefore capital.

(d) Which two items are not classified as liabilities of Blue BBQ?

Item	
Cash paid to repaint the factory	✓
Purchase of goods on credit	
Output VAT on sales	
Money invested into the business by Ron	✓

ANSWERS TO PRACTICE QUESTIONS: **SECTION 2**

TASK 2

(a) What is the name for a budget that remains the same regardless of volume?

Budget	
General budget	
Set budget	
Fixed budget	✓
Determined budget	

(b) If Blue BBQ's actual costs exceed their budgeted costs, what does this represent?

Description	
Favourable variance	
Cost allocation problem	
Variable budget	
Adverse variance	✓

(c) Calculate the percentage variance to two decimal places.

Variance	
1.80%	
3.74%	✓
3.89%	
0.00%	

£48,100 – £46,300 = £1,800. £1,800/£48,100 = 3.74%

(d) What is the budgeted material cost for 20 bottles of hot sauce?

Budgeted cost	
£23.20	
£24	
£44	
£26	✓

Spice cost = £1.20 × 20 = £24. Vinegar cost = £0.10 per 100ml. 20 × £0.10 = £2. Total cost = £26.

KAPLAN PUBLISHING

TASK 3

(a) Which of these items is a common reconciling item in a bank reconciliation?

Item	
Contras	
Unpresented cheques	✓
Transposition errors	
Goods in transit at year-end	

(b) A list of balances owed by individual customers is known by what name?

Name	
Receivables ledger control account	
Customer account list	
Sales account reconciliation	
Receivables ledger	✓

(c) When is a contra made?

Contra	
Where a company is both a customer and supplier	✓
Where a customer takes a discount	
When a supplier gives a discount	
Where a customer is declared bankrupt	

(d) Which of the following would be a debit to the receivables ledger control account?

Transaction	
New cash sales	
Payment received from a credit customer	
New credit sales	✓
Discounts given to customers	

TASK 4

(a) Which of the workers in Blue BBQ are not salaried staff?

Staff	
Factory manager	
Office staff	
Sales staff	
Factory workers	✓

(b) Which of the following could be a disadvantage of doing this?

Disadvantage	
There is an inconsistent labour cost per unit	
Employees have no incentive to produce more units	
Quality could diminish if workers rush to make more units	✓
It discourages efficient work, disincentivising workers	

(c) In a typical 7-hour working day, what is the cost to Blue BBQ of the team?

Cost	
£313.60	
£1,206.10	✓
£1,101.10	
£1,085.00	

Total cost = 1 supervisor for 7 hours, 2 senior staff for 7 hours and 10 juniors for 7 hours
= (£17.30 × 7) + (2 × £15 × 7) + (10 × £12.50 × 7) = £1,206.10

(d) If Joan Ludgate generates new orders totalling £2,000, Ben Haverford generates no new orders and Dennis Meagle generates new orders totalling £3,000, which member of the sales team will earn the most in a month?

Employee	
Ben Haverford	✓
Joan Ludgate	
Dennis Meagle	
All earn the same	

Ben = £3,500. Joan = £2,700 + (25% × 2,000) = £3,200. Dennis = £2,100 + (30% × 3,000) = £3,000

AAT: L2 END POINT ASSESSMENT

TASK 5

(a) Which of the following statements regarding VAT is true?

Statement	
VAT is deducted from the net sales price when recording revenue in the financial statements	
VAT on the sales of sauce can be reclaimed from HMRC	
VAT can be reclaimed on an irrecoverable debt	✓
VAT is owed to HMRC on expenses paid by Blue BBQ	

(b) Which of the following has no impact on the amount of VAT to be paid?

Transaction	
Trade discounts given to customers	
Prompt payment discount taken by customers	
Bulk discounts given on large sales	
All these transactions impact the amount of VAT to be paid	✓

(c) Blue BBQ buys bottles totalling £430 inclusive of VAT at 20%.

What amount and type of VAT is this?

Amount and type	
£71.67 output VAT	
£71.67 input VAT	✓
£86 output VAT	
£86 input VAT	

£430 × 20/120 = £71.67. This is input VAT as it can be reclaimed.

(d) A sales invoice for a credit customer has been entered as a sales credit note incorrectly in the digital bookkeeping system.

Identify the consequence of this error.

Consequence	
The total sales value will be understated	✓
The business may despatch goods that have not been sold	
The total amount owed to payables will be understated	
The business may be paid for goods that have not been sold	

Sales would have been debited rather than credited resulting in an understatement.

ANSWERS TO PRACTICE QUESTIONS: **SECTION 2**

TASK 6

(a) Identify THREE internal controls already in place in the purchases system at Blue BBQ.

> Any of:
>
> Any new suppliers must be requested by the purchasing department and approved by April Wyatt or Ron Knope.
>
> No order above £1,000 can be placed to a new supplier until they have successfully delivered five orders on time and of appropriate quality.
>
> April updates the system weekly to note any changes in prices of goods from suppliers.
>
> April sets automated payments to be made to suppliers just before any prompt payment discounts expire from each supplier.

(b) Identify TWO potential problems that Blue BBQ will avoid by having the controls in place over the purchases system.

> No unauthorised suppliers can be used.
>
> Blue BBQ will not make large payments to suppliers who cannot fulfil the order in terms of time or quality.
>
> Blue BBQ will not suffer from price rises and lose out on good deals if alternative suppliers are cheaper.
>
> Blue BBQ will not miss out on potential prompt payment discounts.

TASK 7

(a) Identify one report prepared by April's team that will be a financial accounting report and one which will be a management accounting report.

> Financial accounting reports – one of:
>
> - Statement of financial position
> - Statement of profit or loss.
>
> Management accounting reports – one of:
>
> - Comparison of units produced in the factory
> - Reports of sales orders per product
> - Reports showing the wastage of ingredients
> - Reports which compare actual results to budgeted results each week.

(b) Using the information on the reports produced by April's team, outline THREE differences in management accounting reports and financial accounting reports. This can be in terms of their preparation, their content, their layout, or how they are used.

> Any 3 of the following areas:
>
> The financial accounting reports are prepared annually, whereas management accounting reports can be prepared whenever requested, whether weekly, monthly or on a more ad-hoc basis.
>
> The financial accounting reports of the statement of financial position and statement of profit or loss have prescribed formats for all companies, whereas the format of management reports will be determined internally, probably by Ron.
>
> The financial accounting reports are prepared for external users, whereas management accounting reports are prepared for internal users, such as Ron.
>
> The financial accounting reports provide a record of the results, but the management accounting reports are requested by Ron in order to make the running of Blue BBQ more efficient.
>
> Some of the management accounting reports will contain forward-looking information, such as budgeted figures, whereas the financial accounting reports show historical results.

TASK 8

(a) What is the name of this other method and how is it calculated?

> The other method is the weighted average cost method (or AVCO). This uses the average cost price per unit with a new average cost calculated before each issue of inventory into production. The average price per unit is calculated by dividing the total value of inventory by the total units in inventory.

(b) In times of inflation, describe which method would give the HIGHEST valuation for inventory and why.

> FIFO (First-in, first-out) would produce the highest inventory valuation in times of inflation. This is because the inventory sold is deemed to be the oldest items, meaning that the year-end inventory balance would consist of the most recently purchased items. In times of inflation, the most these items would be more expensive than those purchased earlier which would give them a higher value.

(c) Identify ONE potential item of work-in-progress that could exist at the end of a week in Blue BBQ.

> The customised products could be WIP at the end of the week, as these take days to produce.

ANSWERS TO PRACTICE QUESTIONS: SECTION 2

TASK 9

(a) Enter the timesheets into the digital bookkeeping system by entering the details of the timesheet.

Employee code	Timesheet number	Number of hours	Rate £	Rate per hour £
915	1167	35	Normal rate	15
915	1167	12	Overtime rate	21

Picklist: Normal rate, Overtime rate

Employee code	Timesheet number	Number of hours	Rate £	Rate per hour £
946	1173	28	Normal rate	12.50

(b) Show how the wages expense will be recorded in the general ledger.

Account name	Amount £	Debit	Credit
201	48,400	✓	
401	48,400		✓

Total = gross wages plus employer's NIC plus employer's pension

TASK 10

(a) Enter the credit note into the digital bookkeeping system by:
- selecting the appropriate menu option
- entering the details of the credit note.

Menu option:

Credit customers – sales credit notes

Customer	Invoice date	Invoice number	Net amount £	VAT £	Total amount £
JWM	28 September	CN163	750	150	900

£900 × 100/120 = £750

(b) Select the correct general ledger codes and show the entries required to record the credit note.

General ledger code	Debit £	Credit £
001	750	
403	150	
402		900

KAPLAN PUBLISHING

TASK 11

(a) Select the correct general ledger codes and prepare entries in the journal daybook to:
- remove the original entries
- record the correct entries.

Journal daybook

General ledger code (picklist)	Debit £	Credit £
604	500	
101	500	
900		1,000
Details: journal to remove the original entries		

General ledger code (picklist)	Debit £	Credit £
604	500	
101		500
Details: journal to record the correct entries		

(b) Identify whether the errors below will lead to the creation of a suspense account or not.

Error	Will create a suspense account	No suspense account created
A purchase of machinery was incorrectly debited to repairs and maintenance expense.		✓
Chris has forgotten to record a journal for an irrecoverable debt.		✓
A petty cash payment of £30 was credited to cash with no other entry made.	✓	
A credit sale of £1,000 was debited to sales and credited to the receivables ledger control account.		✓

ANSWERS TO PRACTICE QUESTIONS: **SECTION 2**

TASK 12

(a) Using the information from Anne's note and the supplier statement above, note the corrections which must be made to the payables ledger.

Error	Amount to adjust £	Debit/Credit
Invoice 24346	**200**	Credit
Invoice 24347	**300**	Credit
Contra	**600**	Credit

(b) What will be the balance carried down in the payables ledger?

Amount £	Debit/Credit
6,400	Debit

Payables ledger

Item	Amount £	Item	Amount £
Payment made	1,200	Balance b/d	1,900
Payment made	1,450	Invoice 24344	1,200
		Invoice 24345	1,450
Goods returned	700	Invoice 24346	2,000
Balance c/d	**6,400**	Invoice 24347	3,200
	9,750		9,750

You need to provide the supplier with the errors in their statement. Complete the table below.

(c) Complete the statement below:

	£
Balance as per supplier statement	7,100
Item	**Error amount**
Goods returned	(700)
Correct balance	6,400

(d) What type of error has been made?

Error type	
Error of commission	
Transposition error	
Error of principle	
Error of omission	✓

KAPLAN PUBLISHING

TASK 13

(a) Prepare entries in the journal daybook to record the
- Bank loan
- Money from Ron.

Journal daybook

Account code	Debit £	Credit £
101	150,000	
405		150,000
Details: Journal to record the bank loan		

Account code	Debit £	Credit £
101	50,000	
701		50,000
Details: Journal to record the deposit of money from Ron		

(b) Which of the following principles will you use to explain this to Anne?

Accounting principle	
Accounting equation	
Business entity	✓
Dual aspect	

(c) Using the information from the list below, total the amounts to be recorded in assets, liabilities and expenses.

Assets £	Liabilities £	Expenses £
216,000	11,500	26,900

Section 3

MOCK ASSESSMENT QUESTIONS

ASSESSMENT INFORMATION

- The total assessment duration is 1 hour and 45 minutes. This **includes 15 minutes** reading time to review the scenario. You may use this time to make notes to help you prepare. You will have 1 hour and 30 minutes to respond to all tasks.

- In your real exam, your invigilator will inform you when you can start your assessment.

- This assessment has a total of 13 tasks.

- The marks available for each task are shown at the top of each task.

ASSESSMENT SCENARIO

- The scenario for this mock exam is based on a fictitious organisation called Pizzaah. The business is a sole trader that sells a range of frozen pizzas and snacks to the major supermarkets in its country. In addition to this, Pizzaah attends a number of festivals and operates food trucks there.

- The scenario can be viewed at any time during the assessment.

- In your real exam it will be made available in every task via pop-up windows which can be opened by clicking on the links on the menu provided to the right of each task.

- In your real exam you can open, close and re-open the pop-ups as often as you wish and position them anywhere in the screen during the assessment.

ASSESSMENT SUPPORT

- Read each task carefully before you start to answer it.

- You can return to a task at any time during the assessment to check your answers

- All tasks are independent. You will not need to refer to your answers from previous tasks.

- Answer the tasks in the spaces provided. For tasks requiring extended written answers, the answer box in your real exam will expand to fit your answer.

- You must use a full stop to indicate a decimal point. For example, write 100.57 not 100,57 or 100 57.

- Both minus signs and brackets can be used to indicate negative numbers unless task instructions say otherwise.

- You may use a comma to indicate a number in the thousands, but you do not have to. For example, 10000 and 10,000 are both acceptable.

- Where the date is relevant, it is given in the task data.

Pizzaah

41 Kansas Way

Bluegrass

BG3 4RT

VAT registration 978 13521 93

Background information

Pizzaah is owned by Michael Schrute, a sole trader. The business sells a range of frozen pizzas and snacks to the major supermarkets in its country. In addition, Pizzaah attends a number of festivals and operates food trucks there. The food is produced in Pizzaah's own factory at Pizzaah's headquarters, where there is a warehouse and an office on-site where all the administration and distribution is managed.

All properties are owned by Pizzaah, but the food trucks are rented under short-term leases of 12 months with the annual rental charge agreed each year.

The factory manager and office staff are paid an annual salary. The factory workers are paid an hourly rate and generally work 35 hours each week.

The food truck staff are also paid an hourly rate, though their hours vary depending on the number of events in any week. Any event for the food truck staff is at normal pay for the first 7 hours, and overtime after this. Overtime also applies to any hours worked on public holidays.

Some of the sales staff receive a commission, in addition to their basic salary, for any large supermarket orders they have generated.

The factory workers submit weekly timesheets to the Finance Department who then process these through payroll. The sales manager submits a monthly report to the Finance Director at the end of every month, with details of orders generated by each member of the sales team in that month.

You are Pam Halpert and work for Pizzaah as a Finance Assistant. Today's date is 1 May 20XX. Your team consists of you and two other Finance Assistants called Dwight Scott and Meridith Bratton and you all report to your line manager, Jan Martinez. Dwight performs a regular review of the prices charged by suppliers for Jan, to ensure Pizzaah is receiving the best deal. Jan has just completed the following reports to send to the Finance Director:

- Number of orders placed per supermarket each month
- Forecast staff costs for May and June
- Pizzas produced each month in the factory
- Monthly profit made from food trucks.

MOCK ASSESSMENT QUESTIONS: SECTION 3

VAT

The organisation operates the standard VAT scheme. All VAT is charged at 20%.

Accounting system

Pizzaah uses a customised digital bookkeeping system. There is a rota system amongst you, Dwight and Meridith to perform daily checks on the entries made.

All suppliers are allocated a code based on the first two letters of their name and a number. All journals are recorded in a journal daybook.

Once a transaction is entered into the digital bookkeeping system, the system will automatically post entries to all relevant accounts. When a journal to write off an irrecoverable debt is entered, the system will also make the necessary adjustment to that particular customer's account in the receivables ledger.

Dwight also compares the bank statements to Pizzaah's cash book in order to check for errors. He does this on a monthly basis. All petty cash payments need a signed voucher, authorised by Jan or another department manager. Dwight replenishes the petty cash system weekly. This process is reviewed by Meridith and documentation is completed to show the amounts reimbursed.

Transactions are entered into the digital bookkeeping system by selecting the menu options. Payments to credit suppliers and receipts from credit customers are recorded using the Credit suppliers and Credit customers menu options. All other payments and receipts are recorded according to the payment method.

These are the menu options you may need to use today:

Main menu	Sub menu
Credit suppliers	Purchase invoices
	Purchase credit notes
	Payments to credit suppliers
Credit customers	Sales invoices
	Sales credit notes
	Receipts from credit customers
Bank	Payments
	Receipts
Cash	Payments
	Receipts
Petty cash	Payments
	Receipts
General ledger	Journal entries

These are the accounting codes you may need to use today:

General ledger code	Account	General ledger code	Account
001	Sales – pizza	601	Rent paid
002	Sales – other frozen	602	Repairs and maintenance
003	Sales – food trucks	603	Gas expense
004	Discounts allowed	604	Electricity expense
005	Purchases	605	Telephone expense
006	Discounts received	606	Motor expenses
101	Bank	607	Water rates
102	Cash in hand	608	Accountancy fees
103	Petty cash	609	Legal fees
201	Factory wages	610	Sundry expenses
202	Office wages	611	Insurance
203	Sales salaries & commission	612	Subsistence
204	Food truck wages	613	Bank charges and interest
205	HMRC liability	614	Irrecoverable debts written off
206	Pension liability	701	Capital
402	Receivables ledger control	702	Drawings
403	VAT control		
404	Payables ledger control		
405	Loan liability		
501	Land and buildings		
502	Motor vehicles		
503	Fixtures and fittings		
504	Plant and machinery		

Payroll information

The payroll details for the sales staff are as follows:

Name of employee	Employee code	Monthly salary	Commission percentage
Oscar Kapoor	1452	£3,100.00	0%
Andy Beesley	1745	£2,350.00	25%
Angela Bernard	1900	£2,800.00	20%

The payroll details for food truck staff are as follows:

Employee function	Hourly wage	Overtime rate (on public holidays)
Chef	£17.30	£24.00
Sales staff	£13.00	£19.00

Other information

Michael is keen to expand the business by increasing orders with supermarkets. To do this, he will need to extend credit terms to major supermarkets in the country.

During your recent appraisal you expressed a keen interest in the payroll function of the business. Jan agreed that as part of your professional development, she would delegate the task of checking the payroll to you.

Pizzaah requires all accounting staff to have up to date knowledge in the areas of accounting systems and processes, bookkeeping controls and recognising and rectifying errors.

Staff must periodically complete a test comprising 13 questions to evidence their continuing professional development in these areas. You have been asked to complete the test today.

TASK 1

(a) Which document will be raised when a customer contacts Pizzaah to place an order?

Document	
Purchase order	
Purchase invoice	
Sales invoice	
Sales order	

(b) Which principle explains that money from Michael Scott is shown as capital?

Principle	
Separate entity principle	
Dual effect principle	
Accounting equation principle	
Capital principle	

(c) Which of the following would there be an impact on where drawings are taken from a business?

Description	
Income and expenses	
Expenses only	
Capital only	
Income and capital	

(d) Which of the financial statements contains all income and expenses?

Financial statement	
Statement of profit or loss	
Statement of financial position	
Statement of changes in equity	
Statement of cash flows	

TASK 2

(a) What is another name for the books of prime entry?

Books of prime entry	
Core files	
Financial statements	
Trial balance	
Day books	

(b) Which type of code is used by Pizzaah for its suppliers?

Type of code	
Sequential	
Alphanumeric	
Alphabetical	
Numerical	

(c) Which of the following is the correct formula for cost of goods sold?

Formula	
Cost of goods manufactured plus opening finished goods less closing finished goods	
Cost of goods manufactured less opening finished goods less closing finished goods	
Cost of goods manufactured less opening finished goods plus closing finished goods	
Cost of goods manufactured plus opening finished goods plus closing finished goods	

(d) Which of the following is a credit balance?

Item	
Gas expense	
Legal fees	
Discounts received	
Purchases	

AAT: L2 END POINT ASSESSMENT

TASK 3

(a) Dwight has budgeted £205,000 of overheads for the next period. Dwight expects Pizzaah to produce 420,000 units. He anticipated factory labour will be 200,000 hours and the machines will be working for 180,000 hours.

What is the overhead allocation on a per unit basis?

Allocation	
£1.03	
£1.14	
£0.49	✓
None of the above	

(b) Pizzaah's equipment can produce food items, 100 at a time.

If they use 100 items as a cost unit, what would the term for that be?

Cost unit	
Batch	✓
Individual job	
Service	
Item	

(c) Dwight budgeted materials cost for a month at £9,600 but they only cost £8,300.

What type of variance is this?

Variance	
Adverse	
Favourable	✓
Unplanned	
Forecast	

(d) Which of these people should Dwight discuss this variance with?

Individual	
Warehouse staff	
Payroll manager	
Sales manager	
Purchases manager	✓

TASK 4

(a) Which of the following payment methods describes an automated regular payment set up for varying amounts?

Payment type	
Standing order	
Direct debit	
BACS	
CHAPS	

(b) What is the name of the process that Dwight performs in comparing the bank statement to the cash book?

Name	
Bank control check	
An ad-hoc procedure	
Sales control account reconciliation	
Bank reconciliation	

(c) Jan has written a cheque for £500 to Dough Co Ltd.

Who is the drawee in relation to this?

Balance	
Jan	
Dough Co	
Pizzaah	
Pizzaah's bank	

(d) What is the name for an item that has been paid into the bank account but does not yet show on the bank statement?

Name	
Outstanding lodgement	
Unpresented cheque	
Deferred cash	
Direct debit	

TASK 5

(a) Which of the following items will be a production cost for Pizzaah?

Cost	
Commission paid to sales staff	
Jan's salary	
Repairs to the factory machinery	
Fuel to deliver to supermarkets	

(b) What is the Economic Order Quantity (EOQ)?

EOQ	
The inventory level, when reached, that required a new order to be made	
Optimal amount of goods to order each time	
The minimum amount of inventory to be held	
The total amount of outstanding orders to be processed	

(c) Which of the following is NOT included in the costs of having inventory?

Cost type	
Purchase price	
Holding costs	
Ordering costs	
Selling costs	

(d) Which of the following statements regarding digital bookkeeping systems is true?

Digital bookkeeping system	
Digital bookkeeping involves storing all records in the cloud	
Digital bookkeeping involves storing all records on a local server	
All digital bookkeeping systems use Microsoft Excel	
Digital bookkeeping systems can import transactions from a variety of sources	

TASK 6

As the finance team has grown, Jan Martinez has been very keen to implement bookkeeping controls.

(a) Identify TWO internal controls already in place over the bank and cash system at Pizzaah.

Jan would like to know the risks that are addressed by these controls and whether any potential risks still exist.

(b) Identify THREE risks that have either been addressed by the controls or that could still exist in the bank and cash system.

TASK 7

Jan has sent her reports to the Finance Director. Meridith is referring to them as financial accounting reports, but all of the reports are management accounting reports.

(a) Explain TWO reasons why the reports would be classed as management accounting and not financial accounting reports.

(b) Identify TWO ways in which Michael may be able to improve the performance of Pizzaah from the food truck report Jan has run.

(c) Explain TWO ways that the other reports may help Pizzaah with planning and motivation in the business.

TASK 8

Pizzaah is looking to improve its inventory systems, as they are worried about the costs of holding too much inventory.

(a) Identify TWO potential problems of Pizzaah holding too much inventory.

Whilst Pizzaah is looking to improve its inventory holding policy, it is aware it needs a buffer inventory for each raw material. Meridith is unsure what this means.

(b) Explain to Meridith what buffer inventory is.

After implementing the new system, Dwight has noted that storage costs for the period are £14,300 compared to a budget of £15,000.

(c) Calculate the percentage variance to 2 decimal places, and identify if the variance is adverse or favourable.

Variance %	Adverse/favourable

AAT: L2 END POINT ASSESSMENT

TASK 9

You have received information from the food truck staff regarding their hours worked in the period. The information below relates to one food truck. Each food truck contains one chef and two sales staff. This needs to be paid immediately from the bank when it has been calculated.

Truck number: 3
Timesheet number: 422

Date	Day of week	Total hours for each person
11.09.XX	Monday (public holiday)	7
12.09.XX	Tuesday	7
13.09.XX	Wednesday	7
14.09.XX	Thursday	8
15.09.XX	Friday	10
		39

(a) Enter the timesheet into the digital bookkeeping system by:

- selecting the appropriate menu option
- entering the details of the timesheet.

Menu option:

Picklist: Bank – Payments, Cash – Payments, Petty Cash – Payments

Employee code	Timesheet number	Number of Standard hours (total staff)	Normal rate £	Overtime hours (total staff)	Overtime rate £	Total pay £
Chef	422		17.30			
Sales staff (×2)	422		13.00			

Angela Bernard's commission has been paid but no entries have been made into the bookkeeping system. Angela made large sales to supermarkets totalling £30,000 in the period.

(b) Process the journal to record the commission in the general ledger

General ledger code	Debit £	Credit £
Details: Journal to remove the missing commission		

Picklist: 101, 102, 103, 201, 202, 203, 204

TASK 10

Michael has taken out a loan to expand the food truck business. Meridith has been made aware that the regular loan repayments made are recorded differently to the loan interest paid.

(a) Using the tables below, show Meridith the double entries that will be required for:
- Loan repayments
- Interest payments

General ledger code	Debit £	Credit £
Details: Entries to record loan repayments		

General ledger code	Debit £	Credit £
Details: Entries to record interest payments		

Picklist: 101, 102, 103, 404, 405, 613

You have been given details of petty cash receipts below. Pizzaah operates an imprest system for petty cash, with an imprest amount of £100. At the start of the week, the amount in petty cash was £100 and the following receipts have been placed in the petty cash box since then:

Date	Type	Amount spent £
11.09.XX	Office supplies	12.00
12.09.XX	Milk	3.40
13.09.XX	Coffee supplies	27.20

(b) Identify how much cash is required to replenish the petty cash box now and whether this will represent a debit or credit to the petty cash balance.

Amount £	Debit/Credit

AAT: L2 END POINT ASSESSMENT

TASK 11

Having made several entries into the digital bookkeeping system you are checking your work when you notice an error. A receipt into the bank from a credit customer of £500 plus VAT has been recorded as a pizza sale.

(a) Select the correct general ledger codes and prepare entries in the journal daybook to:

- remove the incorrect entries
- record the correct entries

Journal daybook

General ledger code (picklist)	Debit £	Credit £
Details: journal to remove the incorrect entries		

Picklist: 001, 101, 102, 402, 403, 701

General ledger code (picklist)	Debit £	Credit £
Details: journal to record the correct entries		

Picklist: 001, 101, 102, 402, 403, 701

One of Pizzaah's suppliers of dough has also ordered some frozen pizzas worth £800. Michael has agreed with the supplier that this amount can be contra'd off rather than paid, but needs you to process the journal to do this.

(b) Process the journal to record the contra in the general ledger.

General ledger code (picklist)	Debit £	Credit £
Details: journal to remove the incorrect entries		

Picklist: 001, 101, 102, 402, 403, 404

TASK 12

Meridith has received all the information required to prepare the VAT control account but has not covered this in her studies. Jan has asked if you can complete this for her, and then Meridith will receive training in the future so she is able to complete it.

Information for the VAT Control account:

Day book – VAT totals	
Day book	**VAT amount**
Sales day book	£4,700
Purchases day book	£2,600
Cash receipts book	£2,800
Discounts allowed day book	£340
Discounts received day book	£150
Purchases returns day book	£250

(a) Complete the VAT Control account below

VAT Control account

Item	Amount £	Item	Amount £

(b) What will be the balance carried down in the VAT control account, and is it payable to HMRC or receivable from HMRC?

Amount £	Payable/receivable

TASK 13

Jan has given you the following totals of some balances correctly extracted at the end of the period. This is not a complete list so will not balance, Jan just wants to ensure you know where each item goes.

Account	Amount £
Sales – pizzas	76,500
Purchases	28,300
Machinery	105,000
VAT Control (credit)	6,400
Loan	60,000
Petty cash	80
Sales – food trucks	18,200
Food truck rental	4,600

(a) Using the information from Jan, calculate the assets, liabilities, income and expenses from the list. Enter all figures as positive values.

Assets £	Liabilities £	Income £	Expenses £

You have been given the following purchase invoice from Sauce Ease, a supplier who offers discounts if Pizzaah pays within 15 days. Jan is unsure whether Pizzaah will pay early or not.

Sauce Ease

VAT registration 446 1532 06

Invoice number 1923

To: Pizzaah   28 September XX

	£
200 of product code S14 @ £8 each	1,600.00
VAT @ 20%	320.00
Total	1,920.00

5% discount if paid within 15 days

(b) Enter the invoice in the digital bookkeeping system by:
- selecting the appropriate menu option
- showing the entries that would be made

Menu option:

[   ]

Picklist: Credit suppliers – purchase invoices, purchase credit notes, payments to credit suppliers

General ledger code	Debit £	Credit £

Details: Entries to record the purchase invoice

Picklist: 001, 005, 101, 006, 403, 404

(c) If Pizzaah pays early and takes the discount, what effect will it have on VAT?

Impact	
No impact	
Reduce VAT reclaimable	
Increase VAT reclaimable	

Section 4

MOCK ASSESSMENT ANSWERS

TASK 1

(a) Which document will be raised when a customer contacts Pizzaah to place an order?

Document	
Purchase order	
Purchase invoice	
Sales invoice	
Sales order	✓

(b) Which principle explains that money from Michael Scott is shown as capital?

Principle	
Separate entity principle	✓
Dual effect principle	
Accounting equation principle	
Capital principle	

(c) Which of the following would there be an impact on where drawings are taken from a business?

Description	
Income and expenses	
Expenses only	
Capital only	✓
Income and capital	

(d) Which of the financial statements contains all income and expenses?

Financial statement	
Statement of profit or loss	✓
Statement of financial position	
Statement of changes in equity	
Statement of cash flows	

TASK 2

(a) What is another name for the books of prime entry?

Books of prime entry	
Core files	
Financial statements	
Trial balance	
Day books	✓

(b) Which type of code is used by Pizzaah for its suppliers?

Type of code	
Sequential	
Alphanumeric	✓
Alphabetical	
Numerical	

(c) Which of the following is the correct formula for cost of goods sold?

Formula	
Cost of goods manufactured plus opening finished goods less closing finished goods	✓
Cost of goods manufactured less opening finished goods less closing finished goods	
Cost of goods manufactured less opening finished goods plus closing finished goods	
Cost of goods manufactured plus opening finished goods plus closing finished goods	

(d) Which of the following is a credit balance?

Item	
Gas expense	
Legal fees	
Discounts received	✓
Purchases	

MOCK ASSESSMENT ANSWERS: SECTION 4

TASK 3

(a) What is the overhead allocation on a per unit basis?

Allocation	
£1.03	
£1.14	
£0.49	✓
None of the above	

£205,000/420,000 units = 49p/unit

(b) If they use 100 items as a cost unit, what would the term for that be?

Cost unit	
Batch	✓
Individual job	
Service	
Item	

(c) What type of variance is this?

Variance	
Adverse	
Favourable	✓
Unplanned	
Forecast	

(d) Which of these people should Dwight discuss this variance with?

Individual	
Warehouse staff	
Payroll manager	
Sales manager	
Purchases manager	✓

KAPLAN PUBLISHING

TASK 4

(a) Which of the following payment methods describes an automated regular payment set up for varying amounts?

Payment type	
Standing order	
Direct debit	✓
BACS	
CHAPS	

(b) What is the name of the process that Dwight performs in comparing the bank statement to the cash book?

Name	
Bank control check	
An ad-hoc procedure	
Sales control account reconciliation	
Bank reconciliation	✓

(c) Who is the drawee in relation to this?

Balance	
Jan	
Dough Co	
Pizzaah	
Pizzaah's bank	✓

(d) What is the name for an item that has been paid into the bank account but does not yet show on the bank statement?

Name	
Outstanding lodgement	✓
Unpresented cheque	
Deferred cash	
Direct debit	

MOCK ASSESSMENT ANSWERS: SECTION 4

TASK 5

(a) Which of the following items will be a production cost for Pizzaah?

Cost	
Commission paid to sales staff	
Jan's salary	
Repairs to the factory machinery	✓
Fuel to deliver to supermarkets	

(b) What is the Economic Order Quantity (EOQ)?

EOQ	
The inventory level, when reached, that required a new order to be made	
Optimal amount of goods to order each time	✓
The minimum amount of inventory to be held	
The total amount of outstanding orders to be processed	

(c) Which of the following is NOT included in the costs of having inventory?

Cost type	
Purchase price	
Holding costs	
Ordering costs	
Selling costs	✓

(d) Which of the following statements regarding digital bookkeeping systems is true?

Digital bookkeeping system	
Digital bookkeeping involves storing all records in the cloud	
Digital bookkeeping involves storing all records on a local server	
All digital bookkeeping systems use Microsoft Excel	
Digital bookkeeping systems can import transactions from a variety of sources	✓

KAPLAN PUBLISHING

AAT: L2 END POINT ASSESSMENT

TASK 6

(a) Identify TWO internal controls already in place over the bank and cash system at Pizzaah.

> Dwight compares the bank statements to Pizzaah's cash book in order to check for errors.
>
> All petty cash payments need a signed voucher, authorised by Jan or another department manager.
>
> Dwight replenishes the petty cash system weekly. This process is reviewed by Meridith and documentation is completed to show the amounts reimbursed.

(b) Identify THREE risks that have either been addressed by the controls or that could still exist in the bank and cash system.

> Dwight's bank reconciliation will prevent errors from being made in the cash book going undetected.
>
> There appears to be no review of Dwight's work so it is possible for Dwight to make an error that goes undetected.
>
> All petty cash vouchers needing a signature should reduce the risk of theft or fraud by people purchasing unauthorised goods.
>
> Managers may simply sign vouchers without checking if the business needs the items, so there could remain a risk, due to the control not being properly implemented.
>
> Meridith's review of petty cash replenishment reduces the risk of Dwight stealing petty cash and trying to cover his own tracks.
>
> There is still a risk that Dwight and Meridith could collude and steal some money together.

TASK 7

(a) Explain TWO reasons why the reports would be classed as management accounting and not financial accounting reports.

> Discussion of any two of the following:
>
> - The reports are used internally rather than externally.
>
> - The reports are focused on the running of the business rather than simply reporting the results.
>
> - The reports are not being something with set rules regarding what must be produced.
>
> - The forecast looks at future costs rather than historical performance.
>
> **Note:** Other valid points may be made.

(b) Identify TWO ways in which Michael may be able to improve the performance of Pizzaah from the food truck report Jan has run.

> Michael can review the profit of individual food trucks and ascertain which locations are most profitable and which are not, to ensure these resources are then directed to the better performing locations.
>
> Michael could review the type of food sold in each unit and ensure that only the best selling products are included in future, removing any unpopular items.
>
> Michael could identify if there are certain dates or times that are more successful and increase the number of food trucks at those times.

(c) Explain TWO ways that the other reports may help Pizzaah with planning and motivation in the business.

> The forecast staff costs will help Michael ensure sufficient amounts are available to pay staff and continue as a going concern.
>
> The number of units produced could be compared month by month, with incentives offered when production increases.
>
> The orders per supermarket could be used to incentivise the sales team to generate more large orders by linking to commission.

TASK 8

(a) Identify TWO potential problems of Pizzaah holding too much inventory.

> Pizzaah is a food producer, so inventory may spoil and have to be thrown away.
>
> There will be higher storage costs, particularly regarding refrigeration and storage of the food items.
>
> There is an increased risk of theft or fraud, and may result in an increased need for security.

(b) Explain to Meridith what buffer inventory is.

> Buffer inventory is the minimum level of inventory to be held. Maintaining this minimum level reduces the risk of running out of inventory.

(c) Calculate the percentage variance to 2 decimal places, and identify if the variance is adverse or favourable.

Variance %	Adverse/favourable
4.67	Favourable

£(15,000 – 14,300)/£15,000 = 4.67%. As the costs are lower than budgeted, this is a favourable variance.

TASK 9

(a) Enter the timesheet into the digital bookkeeping system by:

- selecting the appropriate menu option
- entering the details of the timesheet

Menu option:

Bank – Payments

Employee code	Timesheet number	Number of standard hours (total staff)	Normal rate £	Overtime hours (total staff)	Overtime rate £	Total pay £
Chef	422	28	17.30	11	24	748.40
Sales staff (×2)	422	56	13.00	22	19	1,146.00

The standard hours worked are 4 days (Tuesday to Friday) @ 7 hours/day = 28 days per person. The remainder will be overtime.

(b) Process the journal to record the commission in the general ledger

General ledger code	Debit £	Credit £
203	6,000	
101		6,000
Details: Journal to remove the missing commission		

Angela gets 20% commission, so £30,000 × 20% = £6,000

TASK 10

(a) Using the tables below, show Meridith the double entries that will be required for:
- Loan repayments
- Interest payments

General ledger code	Debit £	Credit £
405	✓	
101		✓
Details: Entries to record loan repayments		

General ledger code	Debit £	Credit £
613	✓	
101		✓
Details: Entries to record interest payments		

(b) Identify how much needs cash is required to replenish the petty cash box now and whether this will represent a debit or credit to the petty cash balance.

Amount £	Debit/Credit
42.60	Debit

£12 + £3.40 +£27.20 = £42.60

TASK 11

(a) Select the correct general ledger codes and prepare entries in the journal daybook to:

- remove the incorrect entries
- record the correct entries

Journal daybook

General ledger code (picklist)	Debit £	Credit £
001	500	
101		600
403	100	
Details: journal to remove the incorrect entries		

General ledger code (picklist)	Debit £	Credit £
101	600	
402		600
Details: journal to record the correct entries		

(b) Process the journal to record the contra in the general ledger.

General ledger code (picklist)	Debit £	Credit £
404	800	
402		800
Details: journal to remove the incorrect entries		

TASK 12

(a) Complete the VAT Control account below

VAT Control account

Item	Amount £	Item	Amount £
Purchases day book	2,600	Sales day book	4,700
Discounts allowed	340	Cash receipts book	2,800
		Discounts received	150
		Purchases returns	250
Balance c/d	4,960		
	7,900		7,900
		Balance b/d	4,960

(b) What will be the balance carried down in VAT control account, and is it payable to HMRC or receivable from HMRC?

Amount £	Payable/receivable
4,960	Payable

MOCK ASSESSMENT ANSWERS: SECTION 4

TASK 13

(a) Using the information from Jan, calculate the assets, liabilities, income and expenses from the list. Enter all figures as positive values.

Assets £	Liabilities £	Income £	Expenses £
105,080	66,400	94,700	32,900

Assets   = Machinery + Petty cash = £105,000 + £80 = £105,080

Liabilities = Loan + VAT Control = £60,000 + £6,400 = £66,400

Income   = Sales of pizza + Sales from food trucks = £76,500 + £18,200 = £94,700

Expenses = Purchases + Food truck rental = £28,300 + £4,600 = £32,900

(b) Enter the invoice in the digital bookkeeping system by:

– selecting the appropriate menu option

– showing the entries that would be made

Menu option:

Credit suppliers – purchase invoices

General ledger code	Debit £	Credit £
005	1,600	
403	320	
404		1,920
Details: Entries to record the purchase invoice		

(c) If Pizzaah pays early and takes the discount, what effect will it have on VAT?

Impact	
No impact	
Reduce VAT reclaimable	✓
Increase VAT reclaimable	

KAPLAN PUBLISHING 123